BUILDING
TRANSFER STUDENT
PATHWAYS

FOR COLLEGE
AND CAREER
SUCCESS

EDITORS
MARK ALLEN POISEL
SONYA JOSEPH

Cite as:

Poisel, M. A., & Joseph, S. (Ed.). (2018). *Building transfer student pathways for college and career success.* Columbia, SC: University of South Carolina, National Resource Center for The First-Year Experience & Students in Transition and the National Institute for the Study of Transfer Students.

ISBN: 978-1-942072-27-0
eISBN: 978-1-942072-28-7 (Ebrary)
eISBN: 978-1-942072-26-3 (EPub)

Published by:
National Resource Center for The First-Year Experience® and Students in Transition
University of South Carolina
1728 College Street, Columbia, SC 29208
www.sc.edu/fye

Production Staff for the National Resource Center:

Project Manager:	Tracy L. Skipper, Assistant Director for Publications
Design and Production:	Allison Minsk, Graphic Artist
	Stephanie McFerrin, Graphic Artist
External Reviewers:	Gloria Crisp, Oregon State University
	Tom Grites, Stockton University
	Barbara Tobolowsky, University of Texas at Arlington

Library of Congress Cataloging-in-Publication Data

Names: Joseph, Sonya, editor. | Poisel, Mark Allen, editor.
Title: Building transfer student pathways for college and career success / Sonya Joseph and Mark Allen Poisel, editors.
Description: Columbia, SC : University of South Carolina, National Resource Center for The First-Year Experience & Students in Transition, [2018] | Includes bibliographical references.
Identifiers: LCCN 2018013869 (print) | LCCN 2018032783 (ebook) | ISBN 9781942072263 (Epub) | ISBN 9781942072287 (Ebrary) | ISBN 9781942072270 (print)
Subjects: LCSH: Transfer students. | Students, Transfer of. | College student orientation.
Classification: LCC LB2360 (ebook) | LCC LB2360 .B85 2018 (print) | DDC 378.1/6914--dc23
LC record available at https://lccn.loc.gov/2018013869

ABOUT THE SPONSORING ORGANIZATIONS ▌

National Resource Center for The First-Year Experience & Students in Transition

The National Resource Center for The First-Year Experience and Students in Transition was born out of the success of University of South Carolina's much-honored University 101 course and a series of annual conferences focused on the freshman year experience. The momentum created by the educators attending these early conferences paved the way for the development of the National Resource Center, which was established at the University of South Carolina in 1986. As the National Resource Center broadened its focus to include other significant student transitions in higher education, it underwent several name changes, adopting the National Resource Center for The First-Year Experience and Students in Transition in 1998.

Today, the Center collaborates with its institutional partner, University 101 Programs, in pursuit of its mission to advance and support efforts to improve student learning and transitions into and through higher education. We achieve this mission by providing opportunities for the exchange of practical and scholarly information as well as the discussion of trends and issues in our field through convening conferences and other professional development events such as institutes, workshops, and online learning opportunities; publishing scholarly practice books, research reports, a peer-reviewed journal, electronic newsletters, and guides; generating, supporting, and disseminating research and scholarship; hosting visiting scholars; and maintaining several online channels for resource sharing and communication, including a dynamic website, listservs, and social media outlets.

The National Resource Center serves as the trusted expert, internationally recognized leader, and clearinghouse for scholarship, policy, and best practice for all postsecondary student transitions.

Institutional Home

The National Resource Center is located at the University of South Carolina's (USC) flagship campus in Columbia. Chartered in 1801, USC Columbia's mission is twofold: to establish and maintain excellence in its student population, faculty, academic programs, living and learning environment, technological infrastructure, library resources, research and scholarship, public and private support and endowment; and to enhance the industrial, economic, and cultural potential of the state.

The Columbia campus offers 324 degree programs through its 15 degree-granting colleges and schools. In fiscal year 2017, faculty generated $254 million in funding for research, outreach, and training programs. South Carolina is one of only 32 public universities receiving both Research and Community Engagement designations from the Carnegie Foundation.

National Institute for the Study of Transfer Students

The National Institute for the Study of Transfer Students (NISTS) exists to improve the lives of transfer students. Through education, research, and advocacy, we support professionals who directly serve transfer students, as well as those who create transfer policy and conduct transfer-related research.

NISTS bridges knowledge, policy, and practice by bringing together a wide range of stakeholders to explore the issues related to the transfer process in order to facilitate student success and degree completion. We partner with two- and four-year institutions, state agencies, higher education associations, foundations, and others committed to transfer student success.

We want transfer and transitioning students to succeed! Our goal is to increase access to and attainment of certificate, associate, and baccalaureate credentials by promoting successful transfer and articulation for two-year, community college, and university students.

CONTENTS

TABLES AND FIGURES

Table

Figure

FOREWORD

Allow me to introduce you to Tevin. He was born in Trinidad and raised by immigrant parents in a small Florida town. His family had little wealth but valued education, and after many years of saving, Tevin was the first in his family to attend college. By his own admission, he was not a good student nor truly ready for college and soon fell prey to an inner dialog that morphed into a sense of hopelessness. Tevin dropped out of college, believing he had failed himself and his family. Fortunately, hitting his lowest point allowed him to be highly receptive to change. He overcame the fear that he would never be good enough, fought back against the perceptions of others, and transferred to a regional institution. There, he soon found a calling in the sciences along with passionate mentors who would guide him to prestigious internships and scholarships. Not only was he named the 2017 Florida Student of the Year, but he is also pursuing a master's degree in biotechnology enterprise and entrepreneurship at a highly selective institution and was recently awarded a $20,000 nationally competitive scholarship. I had the pleasure of meeting Tevin at a STEMconnector Summit this past fall, and he left an indelible mark on me.

Tevin is clearly a superstar who will be the first one to tell you he needed a second chance at an education. You likely know, and have influenced, a student like Tevin who is thriving in higher education and beyond by finding the right opportunity at the right time via transfer. While these students are exceptional, there simply are not enough of their stories to share. Only 13% of the Fall 2010 cohort of community college students earned a bachelor's degree within six years (Shapiro et al., 2017). For some, this was by design; others find their transfer intentions thwarted by a variety of factors including finances, family responsibilities, lack of preparation, and the most poignant of all: a disbelief that success is possible.

Building Transfer Student Pathways for College and Career Success comes to us at a time when more students than ever, with varying levels of success, are choosing to attend multiple institutions of higher learning in search of credentials. This increased mobility is our reality, yet the preponderance of institutions, and the systems that incentivize them, continue to favor direct entry pathways. The past few years have provided access to more accurate and comprehensive national transfer data, allowing us to share the narrative of an often-overlooked critical mass. However, given that transfer remains a predominately local phenomenon, practitioners are challenged to become well versed in enrollment patterns at the state and institutional levels to draw meaningful conclusions about their own transfer populations. Further, dwindling resources lead to a growing dependence on inter-institutional and transdepartmental partnerships to support successful transfer.

Armed with more knowledge, and steadfast in the fundamental belief that transfer provides access to a four-year degree otherwise not achieved, higher education professionals continue to struggle with the tangible *how-tos* that translate transfer intention into reality. Contributing to the challenge is an inconsistent commitment from institutions to assigning professional resources to transfer. While the number of dedicated transfer positions is increasing, many require professionals to juggle additional assignments. Additionally, transfer responsibilities are assigned to entry-level positions that experience high turnover, making it difficult for institutions to create and maintain momentum around transfer. In response to this churning transfer landscape, it is essential to have quality educational resources available for new and seasoned professionals who find themselves in uncharted waters or who want to improve their practice and student outcomes. *Building Transfer Student Pathways* fits the bill. Employing a combination of current research, case studies, theory, and practical application, this collection of carefully curated chapters helps practitioners influence change and intentionally create institutional cultures where transfer students thrive.

Building Transfer Student Pathways is shepherded by two transfer champions whom I have had the pleasure of knowing for many years. Mark Allen Poisel has always prided himself on being "the transfer guy." A passionate advocate whose colleagues learned very quickly that he would introduce transfer into meeting agendas, Mark Allen frequently asked how the important decision on the table would affect transfer students. He would persist until, over time, he was no longer the only one asking the questions, and considerations for these students permeated the culture and decision-making processes. This unwavering passion led us to recruit Mark Allen to serve on the inaugural Advisory Board for the National Institute for the Study of Transfer Students (NISTS), and he has been an incredible asset to our organization, and me, for the past 15 years.

Sonya Joseph quickly became Mark Allen's invaluable "partner in transfer" when he joined the staff of the University of Central Florida (UCF) in 1999. His natural inclination was to reach out to the community college sending UCF the most transfers, and he connected with Sonya, a passionate community college practitioner attuned to creating student-centered policies and procedures that minimize obstacles. From their initial association grew projects related to veterans, curriculum alignment, and student success. On their respective campuses, Mark Allen and Sonya modeled the inter-institutional collaboration necessary to holistically address student success. They carry that same kinship into the pages of *Building Transfer Student Pathways*.

The NISTS team and I have the privilege to bring together transfer professionals from across the country at our annual conference. Year after year, without fail, there is a palpable buzz in the air, an underlying energy. I fondly refer to this as the *transfer synergy effect*—that sensation of feeling connected, the immediate kinship derived from no longer being the lone advocate, the relief experienced when no explanations of complex job responsibilities are necessary. In its presence, our attendees relax, become more receptive to learning, and strengthen their transfer voice. A similar synergy is present in *Building Transfer Student Pathways*. In the pages of this book, you will find support and guidance from like-minded professionals immersed in the study of transfer students and in the practice of supporting them on campus. These individuals combine accessible insights with tangible takeaways to help improve transfer success and strengthen confidence in this meaningful work. Through this rich compilation, Mark Allen and Sonya challenge you to reach beyond what you know and feel confident you can accomplish. They nudge you to use the authors' narratives to further your knowledge, assess your efforts, and redefine transfer success for your students and institution. In these pages, I trust you will find your gem, that concept or program model that speaks to you, and use it to fuel your passion for offering students like Tevin a second chance at an education.

The National Institute for the Study of Transfer Students is pleased to co-publish this book with the National Resource Center for The First-Year Experience and Students in Transition. This collaboration solidifies a long-standing admiration for the work executed by the National Resource Center on behalf of college students and the professionals who so passionately serve them.

Janet L. Marling
Executive Director
National Institute for the Study of Transfer Students
Associate Professor of Education
University of North Georgia

Reference

Shapiro, D., Dundar, A., Huie, F., Wakhungu, P. K., Yuan, X., Nathan, A., & Hwang, Y. (2017, September). *Tracking transfer: Measures of effectiveness in helping community college students to complete bachelor's degrees* (Signature Report No. 13). Herndon, VA: National Student Clearinghouse Research Center.

INTRODUCTION

Mark Allen Poisel and Sonya Joseph

Despite research, institutional programs, and a national agenda focused on transfer students, institutions have not moved the needle for transfer student completion over the past several decades. In 2011, we edited a collection of essays (see Poisel and Joseph, *Transfer Students in Higher Education*) that defined the transfer population and different types of transfer; reviewed policies and practices that welcomed transfer students and their credits; discussed smoother transfer pathways; provided assessment of transfer practices; and challenged institutions to create coherent, viable transfer pathways to support students and align institutional policies to help transfer students graduate. The monograph set the groundwork for continuing discussions of institutional efforts to develop strategies for recruitment, retention, progression, and graduation of transfer students. Since that time, the transfer population has continued to increase. In 2003-2004, approximately one in five students enrolling in four-year institutions for the first time were transfer students (NCES, 2008). A decade later, Simone (2014) reported "about one third of first-time beginning undergraduate students transferred or coenrolled at least once" (p. iv) during the six-year period they were followed. However, only 41% of those students who transfer into a four-year institution pursuing a bachelor's degree actually achieve their goal (Blackwell, 2018).

More than ever, current policy discussions focus on increasing access to higher education and lowering the cost of obtaining a bachelor's degree. Transfer has become an essential component of the educational journey for many students seeking an accessible and affordable bachelor's degree. For the past several years, policy discussions in many states have focused on free tuition at community colleges. As these policies come to fruition (as they have in Tennessee and New York), the transfer population has the potential to multiply exponentially.

Another approach to managing access and affordability has been to increase opportunities to earn college credit and, thus, reduce the time needed to complete a degree. Dual enrollment programs are one strategy for achieving these twin aims. In 2010-2011, there were 1.9 million students taking advantage of dual enrollment programs; this is up from 1.2 million in 2002-2003 (Gewertz, 2016). Other strategies for increasing access and reducing costs include the evaluation of prior learning, early development of career pathways, and the academic preparation of secondary school students.

In 2011, we identified several common transfer patterns (i.e., vertical transfer, swirling, reverse transfer). No doubt, these still exist, but the pathways students take into and through higher education have continued to evolve as states adopt new strategies to increase access and affordability. Students new to a college or university may bring with them credits earned at another postsecondary institution, but they may also bring college credits earned while still in high school. Students entering colleges and universities with credits earned from several sources may be following a graduation pathway that does not necessarily align with the degree requirements of credentialing institutions. The greater national focus on prior learning assessments and experiential credit, whether from the military or industry, creates additional challenges for helping students build appropriate credit toward degree completion.

As such, institutions must evaluate what should be done to help students manage transfer credits in ways that lead to meaningful and efficient pathways to the baccalaureate. Many institutions will need to refocus their missions, values, and expectations about transfers if they plan to make their enrollment an integral part of the college's operations. Faculty and staff will need to be engaged in creating a new vision for all students that includes unique strategies for promoting the retention, progression, and graduation of an increasingly mobile student population. Proven results have come from institutions whose leaders, at the start of the strategic planning process, account for the importance of transfer students as supporting institutional goals. These leaders ensure strategic plans include measures and tactics specifically related to enrollment, partnerships, and curriculum alignment. The performance of transfer students is tracked as intentionally as that of first-year students.

As state legislatures and higher education departments continue to focus on accountability and graduation, opportunities to improve articulation agreements and build pathways from high school to community college to the four-year institution have garnered more interest. Many policy makers are seeking collaborative strategies, such as the WICHE Interstate Passport Initiative, to improve the seamless transfer of students. Embedded within these efforts is the importance of advanced technological systems, which include seamless data sharing across institutional systems (i.e., secondary, two-year systems, colleges and universities) to determine how well students are moving in, through, and out of higher education. This type of data sharing should also include degree audit and educational planning systems. Providing access to these tools at the secondary level will help guidance counselors, parents, and students map college pathways, provide specific information about program requirements, and eliminate the accumulation of excessive credit.

Emerging pathways and technology require different approaches to advising transfer students. Review and evaluation of their current credits must take place during orientation or at the first meeting between advisor and student. What academic plan is the student following? Are the student's intentions the same as when they first began college-level work? Is the student prepared both academically and socially to begin coursework with students already at the new institution?

Institutions may also need to consider what orientation to college should look like for new students entering with varying levels of experience with the college environment. Rather than a single orientation program with a separate session or track for transfer students, institutions may need to offer multiple orientation programs in a range of different modalities to serve the needs of a diverse entering student population. Defining the different transfer populations and determining the needs of each population are key first steps in designing effective orientation experiences.

Programmatic academic initiatives provide structure, resources, and wrap-around services to specifically identified populations, such as underrepresented or underprepared students. Such initiatives are receiving greater emphasis as institutions respond to the need to increase access for underrepresented students and to ensure that these students persist and complete a postsecondary degree. School districts and the local colleges they feed need to explore the extent that pushing a high school curriculum into the middle grades provides greater access to higher education for all students or merely widens the gap for underrepresented students. As institutions continue to move in this direction, curriculum realignment, faculty development, and student support services will go a long way in minding the gap that may have been created by dual enrollment programs for first-generation students and underrepresented students.

A central component to any plan is ongoing assessment and ability to document accountability for achieving set priorities and goals. Defining what success will look like is an essential first step. With respect to transfer student success, outcomes are necessarily defined at the institutional level and could include students seamlessly transferring credits into the institution, achieving a certain GPA, retention, progression toward degree completion, and graduation rates, depending on the population of transfer students served. For some institutions (e.g., community colleges or two-year campuses within state systems), acceptance and matriculation into a four-year institution may be the measure of success. Formative and summative assessment and real-time implementation of evaluation findings are also important when evaluating and communicating the effectiveness of transfer programs.

Strategic plans normally span three to five years or more, and assessment becomes critical for ongoing decision making and possible redirection of plans. As the state and national discussion around transfer students' accountability and success continues, the assessment process plays an important role in providing information that will allow for changes and improved use of results.

Seven years after the publication of *Transfer Students in Higher Education*, the population of transfers continues to expand, as does the conversation about them. Yet little has been done to increase their completion rates or improve their experiences. At the same time, colleges and universities face stagnant or declining enrollments, and calls for greater accountability for transfer student success and completion continue.

The current book refocuses the conversation on lingering issues surrounding transfer and explores those issues emerging in the new transfer context. To that end, this new collection explores the progress institutions have made to create successful programs and pathways for transfer students while posing new questions to better understand the evolution of the work on transfers. The authors also look at new practices and policy changes impacting transfers' success. This volume is organized to provide specific examples and recommendations for college and university professionals who are looking for new approaches to support transfer students and to help institutions enhance their efforts to improve transfer student success. The chapters provide research, case studies, and strategies that lead to best practices at institutions and within state systems.

To help frame the current conversation on the subject, Doug Shapiro describes recent research on the success and mobility of transfer students in the United States in Chapter 1. He focuses on the patterns of transfer and the need for student mobility throughout the pursuit of higher education, underscoring the conditions driving mobility. He highlights the importance of identifying specific outcomes related to transfer students.

Chapter 2 is a case study of collaborative efforts across multiple systems of higher education within a single state. Nancy Dietrich, Gloria Gammell, and India Lane provide perspective on partnerships in the state of Tennessee and how reverse awarding of degrees plays out to increase the number of credentialed residents.

Maria Hesse and Joyce Romano provide two additional approaches to partnerships between community colleges and universities in Chapter 3. Statewide efforts in Arizona and Florida are improving access to higher education while also increasing the number of degrees awarded. Hesse and Romano's chapter describes the very intentional efforts to develop partnership opportunities across multiple sectors to benefit students in these states.

In Chapter 4, Stephanie M. Foote focuses on the research, critical development, and implementation of a transfer-specific orientation program. She highlights some best practices demonstrating the unique and necessary components of an orientation designed with transfer students in mind and the impact such efforts can have on their persistence and progression.

Carol Van Der Karr argues that academic advising plays a critical role in the success of transfer students in Chapter 5. She also provides key factors for implementing successful advising for an increasingly mobile transfer student population.

With Chapter 6, the focus shifts to facilitating success through the emerging pathways and programmatic initiatives campuses have introduced to ease movement along those pathways. Kathleen Plinske argues that *stereotype threat* creates additional challenges for transfer students from underrepresented populations and highlights efforts to help students overcome stereotypes and their impact at one state college.

In Chapter 7, Kristen Moser describes the importance of program and institutional assessment. She explains various models of assessment and how they can be used to measure transfer student success. Moser's chapter also includes the critical aspects of data analysis while highlighting an institutional case study.

The concluding chapter synthesizes and summarizes the ideas presented earlier in the book. As the focus on accountability in higher education increases, there is a greater urgency in addressing the challenges and opportunities for transfer students. Many transfer students focus on the quickest, most cost-effective way to complete their degrees, which may not be the 2+2 model. Students' desired pathways may not align with their institution's traditional routes to degree completion and can impede their successful graduation. With a new emphasis and intentional initiatives, the trend can be reversed so that students follow a pathway that enhances their experience and prepares them directly for their career.

As access points change, colleges and universities will see an increase in the number and type of transfer students. These students will need a wider range of pathways than currently exists; they will also need information about these pathways earlier in their educational journey. Strategic planning, program development, and a deliberate approach to integrating transfers more clearly into the institution will help support degree completion. Making the changes needed for transfer student success will mean reviewing how courses and programs are offered, the needs of an increasingly mobile student body, and the growing diversity of students attending college. Institutions will also need to look for new, nontraditional ways to partner with internal and external constituencies to better support students and institutions. Finally, the combination of the chapters in this book can help practitioners and institutional leaders prepare institutions for work with transfer students and build holistic programs to support their success.

References

Blackwell, M. (2018, April). *The transfer experience at the institutional, state, and national level for student success: Pre-transfer, transfer, post-transfer, and reverse transfer*. Presentation at Valencia College, Orlando, FL.

Gewertz, C. (2016, September 6). Are dual-enrollment programs overpromising? *Education Week, 1*, 12-13.

National Center for Education Statistics (NCES). (2008). *Descriptive summary of 2003-2004 beginning postsecondary students: Three years later* (NCES Report 2008-174). Washington, DC: U.S. Department of Education.

Poisel, M. A., & Joseph, S. (Eds.). (2011). *Transfer students in higher education: Building foundations for policies, programs, and services that foster student success* (Monograph No. 54). Columbia, SC: University of South Carolina, National Resource Center for The First-Year Experience and Students in Transition.

Simone, S. A. (2014). *Transferability of postsecondary credit following student transfer or coenrollment*. Washington, DC: National Center for Education Statistics, U.S. Department of Education.

CHAPTER I
STUDENT TRANSFER AND MOBILITY: PATHWAYS, SCALE, AND OUTCOMES FOR STUDENT SUCCESS

Douglas T. Shapiro

Students in higher education today are increasingly mobile. They move from one institution to another for courses, credits, and programs of study in large numbers, high frequencies, and multiple patterns. The traditional notion of student transfer is a straight, vertical pathway from a two-year college to a four-year school, a way for students to transition from accessible and affordable general education at a community college into advanced study in a major toward a bachelor's degree. Actual student enrollments, however, exhibit much more complex and less focused patterns of behavior. Rather than following a single straight path, today's student journeys often include lateral transfers from one two-year institution to another or among four-year institutions, reverse transfers from four-year to two-year colleges, and many more patterns involving multiple institutions, *swirling back and forth*, and *stopping out* along the way. The traditional transfer pathway is still common but is only one part of the larger phenomenon of student mobility. Institutional practitioners and policy makers serving today's students would do well to understand not just the scale of postsecondary student mobility, but also the varied pathways to degree completion that result when students enroll at multiple institutions over long periods.

The patterns of student transfer and mobility emerge with increasing clarity from a number of studies published during the past four years by the National Student Clearinghouse Research Center.[1] While some of these publications directly address topics of transfer and mobility, not all are focused on transfer per se. Many focus instead on topics such as college completion and time to degree, making it unlikely that transfer professionals will have had the opportunity to read and synthesize the results in the context of their own work. This chapter seeks to fill that gap, collecting insights about student mobility from across the studies.

---

[1] The National Student Clearinghouse is a nonprofit and nongovernmental organization providing educational reporting, data exchange, and verification for more than 3,600 colleges and universities throughout the United States. Here, it is referred to as the Clearinghouse. The National Student Clearinghouse Research Center is the research arm of the National Student Clearinghouse, regularly publishing research on student enrollment, movement, and other important student outcomes using the Clearinghouse's longitudinal data set. Here, it is referred to as the NSC Research Center.

What unifies the recent studies is that each draws upon the Clearinghouse's unique longitudinal data set, which compiles individual student enrollment and degree histories from the student records of the vast majority of colleges and universities in the United States (Dundar & Shapiro, 2016). Looking at the postsecondary education landscape from this vantage point, with the ability to track students' paths across institutions, through time and across states, student transfer and mobility appear more pervasive and varied than the view from a single institution allows. These findings also bring into relief the different outcomes and likelihood of student success to which the more common pathways lead. This information, particularly about the interactions among student mobility behaviors, degree completion, and time to degree, is critical to advisors, institutions, and policy makers seeking to serve the educational aspirations of today's students. Without accurate information about transfer patterns and their likely outcomes, these professionals lack the tools they need to help mobile students plan and anticipate how to reach their goals. They also lack the insights necessary to craft programs and services to meet mobile students' needs.

This chapter outlines postsecondary student mobility, using NSC Research Center reports and findings to demonstrate the magnitude of the phenomenon, its patterns, and some of its effects on student success. It will then focus on how closer attention to data on the range of student enrollment behaviors can help institutions and advisors understand where their students may be coming from before they arrive on campus, where they are going when they leave, and why. Readers will gain insights to better meet students' needs and to increase student success.

Most Students Today Are Mobile

The NSC Research Center uses the word *mobility* to expand the notion of transfer beyond the traditional path. The essential phenomenon of interest is students who enroll at a different institution from where they started, during a time when they are not concurrently enrolled in both institutions. It includes students who may attend only a single term or take a single course at another institution and does not necessarily include a formal transfer of credits from one degree program to another. This classification is important because it captures the behaviors that fully describe how today's students engage with higher education. It also demonstrates the short-sightedness in how institutions often see student choices as limited to either the courses and programs available on campus, or to dropout and failure. For convenience, I will use the terms transfer and mobility interchangeably in this chapter.

The NSC Research Center's *Transfer and Mobility* report (Shapiro, Dundar, Wakhungu, Yuan, & Harrell, 2015) tracked all first-time students who started college anywhere in the fall of 2008 and found that well over one third (37%) had enrolled at a different institution within six years and before earning a bachelor's degree. This number reflects a system-wide view, treating each undergraduate student as a single pathway anchored to his or her starting school. It includes both two-year and four-year institution starters, but in order to avoid double-counting nationally, it counts only the students who transferred out. From the viewpoint of any given campus, on the other hand, the double-counting is the point: The full mobility rate must also include those who transferred in. This addition brings the number to well over half. In other words, over half of all students on a typical campus at any given point in time, on average, are mobile students: They either came from somewhere else, will go somewhere else, or both, before finishing a degree.

This is still not a complete picture, however, because the study tracked students for only six years. Many students take longer than this to earn a degree, and surprisingly many, particularly those who may have stopped out or enrolled part time, make their first transfer after the sixth year. More critically, students often drop out altogether in their first year or even their first term, without ever having much of a chance to transfer. It almost makes no sense to include them in the denominator when calculating transfer rates, given that they neither transferred nor stayed put. One way to address this, and to fully appreciate the scale of transfer and mobility among student enrollment behaviors, along with their role in student success, is to examine enrollment from the finish line as well as the starting line. According to the NSC Research Center's *Time to Degree* report (Shapiro et al., 2016a), roughly 1.5 million students completed a bachelor's degree in the United States in the 2014-2015 academic year. Looking back at their previous enrollments opens up more than 20 years of history—as far back as the Clearinghouse records go and enough to capture the entire postsecondary pathways for nearly every graduate. This method finds that almost two thirds of the students (64.5%) followed mobile pathways, meaning they enrolled in two or more postsecondary institutions on the way to earning their degree. Just over one quarter (25.4%) had enrolled in *three or more* institutions. As remarkable as these numbers are, it is important to emphasize that they represent the successful students—those who completed a bachelor's degree. This means that only about one third of bachelor's degree earners follow the traditional expectation of attending a single college from start to finish, challenging the notion that transfer is somehow a risk behavior confined to those less likely to complete a degree.

Most, but not all, of the multi-institution pathways enumerated in the *Time to Degree* report (Shapiro et al., 2016a) included a community college: More than half (55%) of all the bachelor's graduates, or about 85% of the mobile graduates, had attended a two-year public institution. One in five (20%) of the bachelor's graduates had earned an associate degree. Neither of these facts necessarily mean the students started at a community college, however. Some may have started at a four-year college, enrolled briefly in a two-year institution, and then either returned to the starting school or moved on to another four-year school. Moreover, those who did start at a community college also include students who were dual-enrolled in college while still in high school. The vast majority of high school dual enrollments occur at two-year institutions, and the study counted these students as mobile, too, if they subsequently (after graduating from high school) attended a different college from the dual enrollment school. To indicate how prevalent dual enrollment pathways have become and how important they are to student success, those with prior dual enrollments during high school are estimated to make up about 25% of the total bachelor's-earning class of 2014-2015 in the United States, and 22% of the associate degree earners.

Student mobility is not just a phenomenon of pathways to bachelor's degrees. Even among associate degree earners, a program that many people do not consider to have transfer pathways, almost half (45.4%) of the 573,000 graduates in 2014-2015 had attended more than one college, and 15.5% had attended three or more. As with bachelor's degrees, these multi-institution pathways to an associate degree also include high school dual enrollment patterns, unless the dual and subsequent enrollments all occurred at the same college. Many of the associate degree transfer pathways involved only lateral transfers between two or more community colleges, but others may have started at a four-year institution, or even at a community college, transferred vertically to a four-year institution, and then transferred back to a community college. In these cases, one might reasonably ask whether graduating with an associate degree should be considered a successful outcome. This is but one more variant on the student mobility theme, however, in which even reverse transfers and lateral transfers are important enrollment patterns and success can take many forms as student goals, educational interests, and aspirations change over time.

Few institutions can afford to ignore the students and enrollments represented by these transfer and mobility behaviors. The prevalence and scale of the phenomena should be compelling to any enrollment manager concerned about changing demographics of high school graduates and declining numbers of traditional students. It is not enough to simply recognize all the mobile students whose paths cross the campus each year, whether by transferring in or transferring out, however. Institutions must also learn to better advise and serve these students. The first step is to understand the range of pathways and potential outcomes they pursue, to learn their needs by tracing where they come from, where they are going, and why.

Mobile Student Pathways Are Diverse

It should be no surprise that the large scale of student mobility also gives rise to a diversity of pathways among and through all types of colleges and universities. The range of transfer pathways can best be understood by returning to the vantage point of the starting cohort, where some of the more common pathways, at least, can be more easily described. One of the first assumptions those unfamiliar with the data often make is that most student mobility occurs among those who start at community colleges or other two-year institutions. Results from the *Transfer and Mobility* report (Shapiro et al., 2015) dispel this misconception: Among the 3.6 million students who entered college for the first time in 2008, the six-year transfer and mobility rate for those who started at four-year public colleges and universities is 36.5%, only slightly lower than the 39.5% reported for those who started at two-year publics. Even for those starting at four-year, private nonprofit schools, the rate is 34.3%, still over one third of the starting cohort in the sector.

All told, 1.3 million students from this starting cohort either transferred or enrolled in a different institution within six years, and nearly half (47.7%) had started at a four-year institution. This is important because, while most community college students start out aspiring to earn a bachelor's degree (81% have a degree goal of bachelor's or higher, Horn & Skomsvold, 2011) and would presumably have at least a semblance of a plan to transfer in order to reach that goal, those who transfer out of a four-year institution typically do not do so by design. Little data on the reasons for mobility among students who start at four-year institutions are available, but intuitively these students are likely to transfer for unplanned expediencies, such as issues of affordability, academic difficulty, change of major, poor fit, or any number of nonacademic circumstances affecting domains such as finances, health, family, employment, or even geography. These students may have very different expectations of what constitutes successful degree completion and different needs for guidance and student services than those who transfer as part of a long-term plan.

Another common misconception is that most cases of transfer and mobility involve students transitioning into a four-year institution. In fact, two-year institutions are as much a destination point of student mobility as they are an origination point. Students who started at a four-year school and later enroll somewhere else are about equally likely to go into a two-year as they are another four-year school. The rates are about 49% and 51%, respectively (this, and all remaining statistics in this paragraph, are from Shapiro et al., 2015). To be fair, this includes *summer swirlers* on the two-year side: those who start at a four-year in the fall, take courses at a community college only during summer terms, and return to their starting college the following fall. This phenomenon represents only a small part of the four-year transfer-out population, however. About one eighth of the transfers (13.2% of those who left a four-year public institution and 12.4% of those from a four-year private nonprofit) fit the summer swirl pattern. Another 38% of the transfers from four-year publics went to two-year institutions during a regular fall or spring term and did not immediately return. For private nonprofit institutions, the rate is somewhat lower (30.3%) but still more than twice the number of summer swirlers. Even students who started at two-year institutions, while more likely to transfer to a four-year than to a two-year, nonetheless exhibit a surprisingly high rate of lateral transfer to other two-year institutions. Almost one in six (15.0%) of the starting co-hort transferred to a two-year institution, compared with about a quarter (24.4%) who transferred to a four-year school. In both cases, these numbers represent only the first transfer for each student. Subsequent transfers, for those who moved more than once, could have been at any level. Again, it is important to recognize that each of these different student mobility pathways is likely to carry markedly different kinds of expectations for successful outcomes and different needs for guidance and planning.

Finally, we come to one of the most persistent pathway assumptions, that most transfer students are following the *normal* timeline of vertical transfer. For students starting at community colleges, the expectation that one should spend two years earning an associate degree, followed by transfer and completion of a bachelor's in two more years, persists in the public mind despite all evidence to the contrary. According to data from tracking actual student pathways, at least three facts explain why this particular timeline is not only extremely rare but also highly misleading as a norm.

First, only a tiny fraction, 3.9% of all students who start at community colleges, complete a transfer in the form of a transition to a four-year institution with an associate degree in hand, without any other previous mobility behaviors and within the six-year tracking window of the *Transfer and Mobility* report (Shapiro et al., 2015). Community college students are far more likely either to transfer to a four-year institution without completing an associate degree (21.5%), or, as noted above, to transfer first to a different two-year institution (15.0%)—not to mention the 60.5% who never transfer at all.

Second, even ignoring the part about earning an associate degree, the number who complete a bachelor's degree after just two years at each institution is also surprisingly small. Among all the students who successfully complete a bachelor's degree within six years of starting at a community college, only about 1 in 12 (8.1%) managed to do so by following the 2 + 2 years enrollment pattern (Fink, 2017). Among the pathways to a bachelor's found to be more common than 2 + 2 were: 2 + 3 (17.7% of the graduates), 3 + 3 (13.6%), and 2 + 4 years (10.9%). Notably, each of these common pathways takes more than four years total, and none of them account for more than one in five of just the students who completed within six years. If we were to also include the students who took longer than six years total, the percentage who completed via the 2 + 2 pathway would be even smaller.

These observations lead to the third and perhaps most damaging way in which the traditional time pattern is misleading: When we look beyond the six-year window for starting cohorts and instead consider all degree earners in a graduating cohort, it readily becomes apparent that completing a bachelor's in four years is not a very common pathway under any circumstance, with or without transferring. According to the *Time to Degree* report (Shapiro et al., 2016a), the average bachelor's degree takes about 5.7 years to complete and the average associate degree takes nearly as long: 5.5 years (both measurements are of total elapsed times, including stop-outs). These averages are for all graduates in 2015-2016, with or without transferring and regardless of how many institutions lay in the pathway to the degrees. Among students who enroll at a two-year institution at any point (not necessarily the starting point) in their degree pathway, completing the bachelor's takes even longer: on average eight total years when earning an associate degree first, and six total years with no associate degree. No matter how we look at it, there is nothing common about the traditional transfer pathway to a bachelor's degree, and in the end there simply is no common transfer pathway, traditional or otherwise.

Outcomes for Transfer Students

Seeing the wide range of transfer patterns is helpful in understanding some of the goals and needs of the students moving into and out of institutions today. In order to help students to plan an optimum path and advise them along the way, however, educators need to know the likely outcomes of different pathway options. In this section, we look at the rates of bachelor's degree completion associated with different transfer pathways, with an eye toward informing educators and, ultimately, students, about the efficacy of available enrollment choices.

For example, even though few students manage to transfer to a four-year institution with an associate degree in hand within six years of starting at a community college, earning an associate degree first is not a bad strategy for obtaining a bachelor's if the time limit is extended beyond six years. In fact, out of all students who earned associate degrees in 2010-2011, nearly two thirds (65.1%) enrolled at a four-year institution within the *next* six years, and two fifths (41.4%) earned bachelor's degrees within the same timeframe (National Student Clearinghouse Research Center, 2017a). Of course, as noted above, this is potentially a very long pathway. Adding six years *after* the associate degree onto the average of 5.5 years needed to earn the associate in the first place is not a plan for the student in a hurry. One reason is that many students do not transfer immediately, opting to stop out between the community college and four-year institution enrollments. Almost one fifth (18%) of the students who transferred in 2005-2006 had stopped out for one year or more before entering the four-year college (Shapiro et al., 2013a). That said, it is still a relatively successful plan, especially when considering that even among students who start at public four-year institutions as first-time, first-year students, the overall bachelor's completion rate within six years is only 59.3% (Shapiro et al., 2016b).

As noted earlier, the *Time to Degree* report (Shapiro et al., 2016a) shows that one in five (20%) of all bachelor's degree graduates have previously earned an associate degree. This number has been steadily increasing over the past five years of the report, by about one half a percentage point per year (National Student Clearinghouse Research Center, 2017b). Yet, when looking at the standard six-year window from first entry to graduation, the bachelor's completion rates for all starting community college students are much smaller and the trend is inconsistent: Only 16.0% of students who began at a two-year institution in fall 2010 had completed a bachelor's within six years (with or without an associate degree), compared with 17.8% for the 2007 entering cohort and just 15.1% for the 2009 cohort (Shapiro et al., 2016b). The fact that these rates have not increased more consistently along with the longer-term trend speaks to the complexity of different enrollment pathways and transfer options, and the importance for students and institutions to cut through the confusing signals and focus carefully on individual plans and pathways to success.

We have looked at the bachelor's completion rates for two cohorts: those who start at community colleges and those who earn an associate degree. Yet, for a student embarking on a path to a bachelor's and hoping to start at a two-year institution, some critical points still need clarification. First, it is difficult to know the true intent of students in these cohorts. Responding to a survey question about ultimate educational goals at the time of entry into community college is not the same thing as having a plan to transfer and earn a bachelor's degree. Yet, it does not make sense to measure bachelor's completion rates without filtering out those students who never seriously sought a four-year degree.

An unconventional, but informative solution to improve our understanding of student success rates in this situation is to consider the completion rates for a *transfer* cohort. We can make the starting point the first enrollment at a four-year institution for students who had previously started at a community college and track their bachelor's outcomes for six years from that point of transfer. The *Baccalaureate Attainment* report (Shapiro et al., 2013a) takes this approach. Among the findings are that 61.6% of all students who transferred to a four-year institution in 2005-2006 (with or without an associate degree) had completed a bachelor's degree six years later, in 2012. That is a remarkably high graduation rate for community college students, and yet, measured at six years from the point of transfer, it holds out a distant promise to students setting out on this path. The real value of the report is not in this overall number, but rather in the ability to compare the different pathways the students followed both before and after transfer.

For example, students who transferred with an associate degree were more likely to complete a bachelor's (71.6%) than those who transferred without a degree (55.9%). It may have taken them longer, as observed above, but they were more likely to finish in the end. It is perhaps disconcerting, then, that far fewer students pursued the more successful pathway: about 116,000 of the transfer students had completed an associate degree before transferring, compared with 205,000 who had not. This raises the question of whether students might have chosen their pathway differently had they known the odds. The report also found that the type of four-year institution transferred into made a difference as well, with 64.8% of the students who transferred to a public college or university completing a bachelor's, compared with 60.2% of those who transferred to a private nonprofit institution. While not a large difference, it is striking because it indicates an optimal enrollment pathway that is the opposite of what would be recommended if students were to heed only the official six-year graduation rates for first-time full-time students at four-year institutions, which are lower for those starting at public institutions (57.7%) than at private nonprofits (65.3%, NCES, 2015). Students may rightly consider many other factors when choosing a transfer institution, of course, but having no data points available about the relative odds of success specific to the student's current starting point unnecessarily constrains the decision process.

In another example, the report (Shapiro et al., 2013a) finds that students who stopped out and delayed transferring for one or more years after their last enrollment at a two-year institution had much lower bachelor's completion rates (40.0%) than those who transferred immediately, within one year or less (66.3%). This is one of the largest differences observed in the study, although it is somewhat mitigated by the fact that an additional 12.3% of the stop-out students were still enrolled at the end of the six-year period, compared with only 6.8% for those who had not stopped out. Transferring immediately to a four-year institution may not be an option for many students, and stopping out may be more of an indicator of other risk factors rather than a cause of lower completion odds in itself. As a descriptive study, none of the correlations identified can be interpreted as causal without further research. Nonetheless, for students considering taking time off before transferring who do have a choice, it makes sense that a loss of momentum might lead to an increased risk of struggle later on. Either way, it is information a transfer advisor should be able to access when helping a student plan a pathway from among many possible options.

As a final example of the difference in student degree outcomes associated with transfer and mobility pathways, we consider the case of high school dual enrollment. In the *Completing College* report (Shapiro, Dundar, Ziskin, Yuan, & Harrell, 2013b), the NSC Research Center compared the college completion rates of former dual enrollment students (those who took college classes while still in high school, but whose first post-high school enrollment was in fall 2007) with true first-time students in fall 2007, of similar age, but who had no prior dual enrollments.[2] Not surprisingly, former dual-enrolled students are more likely to finish a degree. Their college completion rate after six years was 66%, compared with 58% for the students with no prior dual enrollment.

The promise of dual enrollment also involves shortening the pathway to a degree. In the *Time to Degree* report (Shapiro et al., 2016a), the data bear this out, as well. Among students who earned an associate degree in 2015-2016, those with prior dual enrollments took, on average, over a year less in total elapsed time to complete the degree than those without. They spent only about one semester less in actual enrolled time, however, suggesting that while they clearly had less academic ground to cover than their peers, thanks to credits earned while still in high school, this alone did not account for all of the difference in elapsed time. They also were less likely to stop out along the way. Although the differences are less pronounced, similar patterns hold for bachelor's degree earners: Students with dual enrollments took about a half a year less in total elapsed time, but only about half a semester less of enrolled time.

In both cases, the degree pathways for many students may have been indirect even after dual enrollment. It is likely, however, that the students who went straight from high school to a four-year institution would have seen a lower acceptance rate of their dual credits than did students who stayed at the community college level after high school, and particularly those who stayed at the same community college. This may help explain the smaller difference observed among the bachelor's degree earners. It is also an important piece of information for students and their advisors to consider when choosing the dual enrollment pathway.

_____

[2] In this case, no distinction is made between those whose fall 2007 enrollment was at the same college or a different college from their dual enrollment. Other researchers using Clearinghouse data have found that among all high school students who were dual enrolled at community colleges in fall 2010, 47% went on to attend a community college immediately after high school, and 84% of those students re-enrolled at the same college where they had dual enrolled (Fink, Jenkins, & Yanagiura, 2017).

Advising, Planning, and Serving Mobile Students

For many students, mobility and transfer behaviors involving multiple postsecondary institutions on the path to a degree are not choices. They are the inevitable results of complex lives, family obligations, strained finances, challenging schedules for work and commuting, and other logistic factors that can force a student to change institutions, stop out, or leave higher education altogether. For other students, enrollment choices might be an accurate descriptor, particularly in the case of savvy education consumers, who are shopping for the optimal path of lowest cost, best academics, and campus amenities combined with the highest value of the degree in the labor market. Or, to offer another type, for young students executing an honest course correction after having made immature choices about institutional fit or major when they simply did not know what to expect or what they were getting into. As each of these scenarios illustrates, however, the ability to anticipate the road ahead, set appropriate goals, and plan accordingly is a basic student need.

Even for the most traditional student, a recent high school graduate, the task of planning a path to a bachelor's degree is not an easy one. This student and their parents are confronted not only with finding the best academic and cocurricular fit but also with balancing that fit, and the value of the education received, against the direct costs, the opportunity costs, and typically, financial aid and financing needs as well. The complexity increases dramatically when the options are expanded to include multi-institution pathways, yet this is also where common sources of guidance often break down. The results described in this chapter illustrate the wide range of pathways traversed by mobile students, as well as some of the different outcomes that can be expected from choices made along the way, but this information is not widely distributed. High school counselors and college and university admissions offices provide valuable information about academics, cost, and financial aid on individual campuses, but information about potential transfer pathways to or from other campuses, including how long it will likely take to complete a program, how much it will cost, and the odds of completing a degree program, is much harder to come by. Starting at a community college and transferring may be an attractive money-saving strategy, for example, but not if an extended time to degree and lost credits add unexpected costs and jeopardize transferring, or even graduating altogether (Belfield, Fink, & Jenkins, 2017). The difference between a degree path lasting four years and one of six, seven, or eight can upend any family's plan to finance a student's education, making this kind of information critical to the planning process.

Students and their families need to know about enrollment strategies that combine offerings from multiple institutions. The results in this chapter are examples of the minimum level of information that advisors should be able to offer mobile students in portraying the new realities of postsecondary education. They represent the most expansive and current data available on how students are navigating transfer pathways to pursue and accomplish their educational goals, but more work is needed. The reports from the NSC Research Center address mobile pathways only in broad strokes, providing little information about the outcomes of transfer pathways at specific institutions.[3] Federal data that are institution-specific, such as the outcomes available on the U.S. Department of Education's College Navigator and College Scorecard websites, cover single-institution enrollment paths only. This means that students and their advisors can weigh the advantages and risks of mobile educational pathways involving different types of institutions, but there is little to guide them in choosing among individual colleges. One notable exception is the Student Achievement Measure (SAM), a collaborative effort by six higher education associations that provides a platform for member institutions to voluntarily report outcomes metrics for students who follow transfer pathways. Currently, more than 600 colleges and universities participate in SAM, with searchable results on an annually updated public website (studentachievementmeasure.org). Individual institutions that measure the outcomes of their own mobile students can facilitate the planning process for prospective students and their advisors by posting their results to SAM. They can also go further, by making the data for specific transfer-sending or transfer-receiving colleges available through their own admissions offices and student advising centers.

Providing better data and consumer-type information for planning and advising is just one part of helping mobile students succeed. Institutions must also find ways to serve mobile students with the kinds of transfer policies and program offerings that meet their needs and further their goals. This begins with recognizing that the many students who pass through campus either after, or before, enrolling somewhere else, deserve an educational experience that respects their past choices and future plans. While they may not fit the traditional student mold, the time these students spend on each campus along their path should meaningfully advance their progress to a degree, with minimal friction due to lost credits, redundant requirements, or policies that ignore their circumstances. Institutions should work to better understand these circumstances and the needs they engender, by combining existing data on mobile pathways with the specific outcomes of their

---

[3] It is a condition of the NSC Research Center's use of Clearinghouse data that no institution may be identified in published results without the express permission of the institution (Dundar & Shapiro, 2016).

own students at key transfer-sending and transfer-receiving institutions. These efforts will generate insights into the conditions and expectations that motivate students to pursue mobile pathways and help inform policies and services that advance success at each point along their pathway.

Note on the Data Sources

In reading these results, it is important to understand just how comprehensive the data source is. The reports by the NSC Research Center cited in this chapter take advantage of the Clearinghouse's unique collection of enrollment and degree records at the individual student level. The data behind these records include all students, from the traditional example who attends full time and starts immediately after high school; to the adult learner who starts after years in the workforce and enrolls part time while raising a family; to the student whose path encompasses both of those patterns, stopping out into the workforce after an initial period of traditional-age enrollment and returning later as an adult. The data include many students, in other words, who are not commonly studied but who make up a growing share of enrollments for many institutions.

The data behind the NSC Research Center reports are also not created from the typical student or institutional surveys using small representative samples, nor do they rely on aggregating the surveys that colleges send annually to the Integrated Postsecondary Education Data System (IPEDS). Instead, the Clearinghouse's comprehensive administrative data collection effectively covers the entire student population. Student-level enrollment data files are submitted to the Clearinghouse multiple times per term by each of the thousands of participating institutions. These colleges and universities currently enroll about 97% of all students in Title IV-eligible, degree-granting institutions of higher education in the United States. The data enable every enrollment instance at any institution to be linked by a student, creating a complete postsecondary pathway at the student level, from first enrollment to final degree, across all types of institutions. (More information on this data source, its origin, structure, and uses, as well as the NSC Research Center's use of the data, can be found in Dundar & Shapiro, 2016.)

References

Belfield, C., Fink, J., & Jenkins, D. (2017). *Is it really cheaper to start at a community college? The consequences of inefficient transfer for community college students seeking bachelor's degrees* (CCRC Working Paper No. 94). New York, NY: Community College Research Center, Teachers College, Columbia University.

Dundar, A., & Shapiro, D. (2016). *The National Student Clearinghouse as an integral part of the national postsecondary data infrastructure* (Creating a Thriving Postsecondary Education Data Infrastructure in the 21st Century No. 8). Washington, DC: The Institute for Higher Education Policy.

Fink, J. (2017, May 8). Visualizing the many routes community college students take to complete a bachelor's degree [Web log post]. Retrieved from https://ccrc.tc.columbia.edu/blog/visualizing-many-routes-bachelors-degree.html

Fink, J., Jenkins, D., & Yanagiura, T. (2017, September). *What happens to students who take community college "dual enrollment" courses in high school?* New York, NY: Community College Research Center, Teachers College, Columbia University. Retrieved from https://ccrc.tc.columbia.edu/publications/what-happens-community-college-dual-enrollment-students.html

Horn, L., & Skomsvold, P. (2011, November). *Community college student outcomes: 1994–2009* (NCES 2012-253). Washington, DC: U.S. Department of Education. Retrieved from http://nces.ed.gov/pubs2012/2012253.pdf

National Center for Education Statistics (NCES). (2015). *Digest of education statistics.* Washington, DC: U.S. Department of Education. Retrieved from https://nces.ed.gov/programs/digest/2015menu_tables.asp

National Student Clearinghouse Research Center (2017a, Summer). *Snapshot report – Certificate and associate degree pathways.* Herndon, VA: Author. Retrieved from https://nscresearchcenter.org/snapshotreport-certificateassociatedegreepathways29/

National Student Clearinghouse Research Center (2017b, February). *Undergraduate degree earners report, 2015-16.* Herndon, VA: Author. Retrieved from https://nscresearchcenter.org/undergraduatedegreeearners-2015-16/

Shapiro, D., Dundar, A., Wakhungu, P. K., Yuan, X., & Harrell, A. (2015). *Transfer and mobility: A national view of student movement in postsecondary institutions, fall 2008 cohort* (Signature Report No. 9). Herndon, VA: National Student Clearinghouse Research Center.

Shapiro, D., Dundar, A., Wakhungu, P. K., Yuan, X., Nathan, A., & Hwang, Y. (2016a, September). *Time to degree: A national view of the time enrolled and elapsed for associate and bachelor's degree earners* (Signature Report No. 11). Herndon, VA: National Student Clearinghouse Research Center.

Shapiro, D., Dundar, A., Wakhungu, P. K., Yuan, X., Nathan, A., & Hwang, Y. (2016b, November). *Completing college: A national view of student attainment rates, fall 2010 cohort* (Signature Report No. 12). Herndon, VA: National Student Clearinghouse Research Center.

Shapiro, D., Dundar, A., Ziskin, M., Chiang, Y., Chen, J., Harrell, A., & Torres, V.

(2013a, August). *Baccalaureate attainment: A national view of the postsecondary outcomes of students who transfer from two-year to four-year institutions* (Signature Report No. 5). Herndon, VA: National Student Clearinghouse Research Center.

Shapiro, D., Dundar, A., Ziskin, M., Yuan, X., & Harrell, A. (2013b, December). *Completing college: A national view of student attainment rates, fall 2007 cohort* (Signature Report No. 6). Herndon, VA: National Student Clearinghouse Research Center.

CHAPTER 2

THE TENNESSEE REVERSE TRANSFER PROGRAM: A CASE STUDY ON PARTNERSHIPS TO SUPPORT SEAMLESS TRANSFER

Nancy Dietrich, Gloria Gammell, and India Lane

Student transfer naturally requires institutions to step outside their boundaries and work with at least one other institution. Partnerships are strengthened when two or more institutions coordinate curricular pathways, advising collaborations, and communications with students. Most commonly, the strongest partnerships lie in pairs of institutions in close proximity and focus on students transferring credits "forward" to keep working toward a degree, either between similar institutions or from a two-year to a four-year institution. Less commonly, students transfer from a university to a community college for the opportunity to complete a shorter degree program, historically designated as *reverse transfer* (Townsend & Dever, 1999). Over the past few decades, student mobility through college transfer has become more complex and increasingly indicates that progression to degree is not always clearly defined.

The contemporary definition of reverse transfer (also known as reverse credit transfer, backward credentialing, or reverse articulation) recognizes progress by allowing a community college student who transfers to a four-year institution prior to earning an associate degree to complete that degree while continuing to work toward the baccalaureate (Friedel & Wilson, 2015; Taylor, 2016). Credits earned at the university are transferred back to the community college to fulfill degree requirements not met prior to transfer. Momentum for contemporary reverse transfer has grown based on the knowledge that completion of an associate degree correlates with increased bachelor's degree completion, though not necessarily by reverse transfer. Additionally, the associate degree may be a useful workforce credential whether the student is progressing toward another degree or stops out. Reverse transfer awards thus enhance community college completion, may motivate toward persistence and completion in four-year institutions, and provide a credential for some students who otherwise would have some college credit but no degree. As of 2015, 13 states had enacted or were considering legislation related to reverse transfer (Garcia, 2015). Friedel and Wilson (2015) described developing or strong participation in reverse transfer in 32 states. Although completion outcomes of large-scale efforts are still emerging, enhanced associate degree completion appears common in strongly engaged states (Taylor, 2016), including Tennessee, where the program leads to about 900 new degrees each year.

Committing to work together throughout the many pathways to a degree, including reverse transfer, helps minimize competitive and territorial barriers that impact student completion, especially when the commitment extends across the entire state. In this case study, the authors describe the partnerships involved in creating the Tennessee Transfer Pathways, the evolution of these partnerships through development of the Tennessee Reverse Transfer program, and the impact of these partnerships on the ongoing, statewide approach to transfer solutions.

Tennessee's Transfer and Completion Landscape

Tennessee consistently falls below the national average in educational attainment (Lumina Foundation, 2017). Fortunately, the state's government, higher education, and business communities recognize that postsecondary education feeds job creation and opportunities, quality of life for individuals, and economic growth for the state. In 2010, lawmakers crafted legislation focused on enhancing educational success. The Complete College Tennessee Act (CCTA) of 2010 mandated a statewide educational master plan, outcomes-based public funding, universal transfer paths, dual admissions programs, and transformed remediation courses.

Spurred by this legislative action, the entire Tennessee educational community has engaged in collaborative, concerted partnerships to better prepare high school graduates for higher education and college graduates for the world of work. Until 2017, the higher education community was organized into three systems: the University of Tennessee (UT) system, with four universities, including a health science center; the Tennessee Board of Regents (TBR) system[4], with six universities, 13 community colleges, and 27 diploma- and certificate-granting colleges of applied technology; and the Tennessee Independent Colleges and Universities Association (TICUA), which services 34 nonprofit, regionally accredited institutions. The Tennessee Higher Education Commission (THEC) serves as the state's higher education executive office and oversight body. While TICUA institutions are not required to join state-mandated programs, many have elected to participate. Leaders of the three systems committed to work hand in hand on the requirements of CCTA as a united group, a philosophy that persists.

---

[4] Since the implementation of Tennessee Transfer Pathways and Tennessee Reverse Transfer, the governor enacted legislation (Focus Act) to reorganize the Tennessee Board of Regents. Effective Fall 2017, the six TBR universities operated independently of TBR and with their own governing boards.

Shared goals are the foundation of the partnerships. These goals include easing the process of transfer throughout the state's public and private colleges and universities, encouraging near-completers to return to college and obtain a degree, providing consistent and rigorous means for awarding prior learning credit, and increasing retention and graduation rates while decreasing time to completion. The key initiatives related to articulation and transfer included establishing common transfer pathways, developing a reverse transfer program, and clarifying policy and procedure for transfer of prior learning assessment (PLA) credit.

In 2013, Tennessee Governor Bill Haslam raised the attainment stakes by launching the highly visible Drive to 55 campaign. The goal of the campaign is for 55% of adult Tennesseans to attain a college degree or certificate by the year 2025, a goal that requires not only efforts to graduate current and future students but also to promote associate or baccalaureate degree completion by adults with some college credit yet no credential. Thus, Drive to 55 became the rallying cry of subsequent educational programs and partnerships to further postsecondary efforts.

Tennessee Promise, the governor's high-profile initiative that provides last-dollar scholarships for community colleges and select four-year schools offering associate degree programs, also raised the stakes for higher education partners in the state. High school seniors who complete the Tennessee Promise requirements are eligible for state funds that cover tuition and fees not funded by federal dollars or other programs. Additional fees, books, and living expenses are not included in the funding. Because some students who might have enrolled in four-year institutions now choose to start their path at a community college, universities are even more invested in attracting and serving upper-level transfer students. Both two- and four-year institutions are gearing up to serve the changing student population as Tennessee Promise fully unfolds.

Subsequent to Tennessee Promise, two statewide programs were developed and implemented in partnership, the Tennessee Transfer Pathways and Tennessee Reverse Transfer. These programs illustrate the importance and value of statewide partnerships.

The Foundation: Tennessee Transfer Pathways

Like other states, Tennessee also has an active, multidirectional transfer landscape. In the 2016-2017 academic year, more than 28,000 students transferred throughout Tennessee institutions. Roughly 10% of the undergraduate enrollment at public colleges and universities is composed of new transfer students. Among Tennessee public university graduates, almost half have changed schools at least once during their baccalaureate program and about one third previously attended a Tennessee community college (THEC, 2017).

The first tangible mission of the CCTA was to craft universal transfer pathways. The Tennessee Transfer Pathways (TTP, www.tntransferpathway.org) are 60-credit hour community college-to-university transfer paths in the most common academic majors. These pathways include specific course requirements. Upon completing a pathway, the student is awarded the appropriate associate degree and is academically prepared to transfer to a participating four-year institution at the junior level. Students complete their final two years of baccalaureate coursework at the four-year institution. Because Tennessee universities were obligated to accept transfer courses within these pathways, the university community was a willing participant and partner in developing each pathway. The UT and TBR system academic affairs leaders solicited faculty nominations and facilitated intensive day-long, discipline-specific meetings to focus on developing and revising pathways. Chosen course selections and options were then circulated to academic leadership and other faculty for comment.

Initially, 40 transfer pathways were developed and implemented in 2012. More are added annually, and student participation in the pathways has grown. These clearly defined common pathways give students a road map for degree completion and are designed to decrease time to the baccalaureate degree. Faculty committees review pathways on a five-year rotating cycle, and students and participating institutions do so at other times as needed. Two- and four-year faculty have dedicated many hours and shared expertise and experience to develop transfer pathways in their respective disciplines.

Relevance of Partnerships

Legislation and campaigns from the governor's office are just the beginning of successful initiatives. Partnerships among the various higher education entities are vital to the success of all statewide initiatives, policies, and programs. To facilitate collaborative efforts for these massive undertakings, statewide intersystem partnerships were developed within the higher education community.

In April 2010, system academic leaders established a statewide Articulation and Transfer Council. It included wide representation in the form of college and university leaders, campus academic administrators, faculty members, and trustees. The council has tackled the overall challenge of managing articulation in the state, whereas individual system leadership has taken the role of staffing the transfer pathway groups and discussions. The council oversees, facilitates, and mediates development of the transfer pathways and has evolved to be an effective advisory group on policy and practice. The current council, which meets annually, includes individuals from THEC, UT, TBR, the six independent public universities, and

TICUA. Members represent institutional administration, admissions, academic advising, records/registrar, and retention personnel.

The council's diversity brings a breadth and scope of experience crucial to successfully developing student-centered programs and policies. Administrators support transfer programs by providing campus resources, while campus representatives serve as information conduits and champions of the programs at their institutions and within their professional state organizations. Their direct involvement and commitment to the programs foster a sense of ownership. THEC representation has been critical to data review and in advancing support through the state legislature and the Office of the Governor. The time, energy, and good will tapped to develop and sustain these partnerships stands behind the success of Tennessee higher education programs.

The Next Piece: Tennessee Reverse Transfer

Enrollment in transfer pathways was slow initially; however, additional work on guided pathways, advising, and four-semester curriculum maps led to rapid increases in students in TTP in academic years 2016-2017 and 2017-2018. Despite these maps and pathways, however, many students still transfer prior to receiving an associate degree. Many will not complete the four-year path, leaving them with no college credential—despite having a baccalaureate degree as an educational goal. For 2015-2016, less than 20% of new transfer students at Tennessee public institutions had earned an associate degree before the time of transfer, including many with more than 60 credit hours earned. In reviewing data prior to 2010, 69% of community college transfers without an associate degree did not complete a baccalaureate degree. While completion is still challenging, transfer students who have earned the associate degree are more likely to persist to graduation.

Opportunities to award the associate degree by reverse transfer have risen in prominence. These awards, which combine credits earned at the previously attended community college and credits earned at the university along the way to a baccalaureate degree, are designed to recognize achievement and provide motivation to complete the bachelor's degree. They also offer a postsecondary credential that can be useful to non-completers. In Tennessee, the General Assembly passed enabling legislation in 2012 that encouraged public institutions to create reverse transfer policies and programs. In the same time frame, the Lumina Foundation launched its Credit When It's Due initiative and offered support for state-level efforts in reverse transfer.

Under the auspices of the Articulation and Transfer Council, Tennessee formed a Reverse Transfer Task Force to explore the value and policy implications of such a program. Members were carefully selected to include needed areas of expertise while also maintaining a balance of representatives from public, private, university, and community college entities. The expertise required was broad, from records and graduation specialists, to technological support, to policy and data analysts. Unlike the development of the TTP curricula team, the task force needed representation from the professional staff sector at schools rather than faculty in the disciplines. Not only were those areas of expertise needed, but so was their commitment to and ownership of the program. The program's magnitude required enormous cooperation and buy-in among the users of the process. Working groups were created from the full task force to tackle issues of policy, technology, cost, marketing, and research goals.

The UT and TBR systems initially staffed the task force, but when funding was secured from a Credit When It's Due grant and state resources, a project coordinator and a part-time community college liaison were selected. The project coordinator was responsible for communications, training, meetings (in-person or via technology), reports (to taskforce members and the council), and general day-to-day oversight. The community college liaison provided key insight into the program's development and enhancement, as well as communicating with records officers in the community college system.

Most reverse transfer programs rely on agreements between a university and one or more local community colleges; the four-year institution agrees to periodically share a transfer student's updated transcript information until their accumulated credit history meets degree requirements. Because college completion was a prominent statewide goal, the task force took a unique and ambitious approach. Instead of encouraging pairs of institutions to initiate and manage the credit exchange, twice each year student enrollment and course completion data from participating universities are compared with enrollment data for all community colleges in the state. Initial screening degree audits, based on community college requirements, are run for all matched students. The statewide approach enabled rapid scaling of the program and ensured equitable participation among public institutions.

Policy Development

After initial discussions and fact finding by the task force, the policy workgroup focused on a framework for the governing policies. The group reviewed existing policy from other states already awarding reverse transfer degrees, relevant accreditation standards, and existing Tennessee transfer and graduation policy. Later, the project director and community college liaison prepared a draft policy that was reviewed and recommended by the task force for adoption. In

June 2014, the council reviewed, edited, and approved the Reverse Transfer Policy Recommendations.

Using the five dimensions of reverse transfer delineated during the Credit When It's Due initiative (Taylor & Bragg, 2015), the key elements of the Tennessee policy include the following:

- **Student identification** is initiated at the four-year institution. Enrolled transfer students are considered for Tennessee Reverse Transfer if the student has completed at least 15 credit hours at a participating Tennessee associate degree-granting institution and earned at least 60 cumulative credit hours.

- Affirmative **consent** is obtained and held by response to an automated, centrally generated email.

- Course histories are uploaded to a central database for initial screening analyses; final **transcript exchange** for official records purposes is managed by the institutions.

- A simulated **degree audit** is also completed centrally; however, the community college awarding the associate degree reviews the audit results and may complete additional formal audits. The reverse transfer policy allows for the substitution of selected upper-level courses for community college requirements.

- **Degree conferral** is the purview of the community college, and final notification of the award is the responsibility of the community college. Colleges are also encouraged to provide follow-up **advising** for students who do not yet meet the requirements for the associate degree regarding course deficiencies and the most effective path to earning a credential.

The taskforce decided to limit the initial reverse transfer degree awards to the 40 established transfer pathways because (a) community college graduation audit analysts and four-year advisors were already familiar with degree requirements; (b) the number of degree tracks would be manageable; and (c) since students had been encouraged to complete a pathway, it seemed logical that the likelihood of reverse transfer degrees built on the pathways would be high. Additionally, at the two-year institutions' request, a general studies associate degree was included (general education requirements and additional elective courses). As additional transfer pathways were developed, they were added to the reverse transfer awards.

Putting Policy into Practice

A technology workgroup tasked with exploring existing reverse transfer systems as well as the feasibility of internal development determined that partnering with a commercial vendor (AcademyOne Inc.; Philadelphia, PA) was the most efficient route to a successful audit system. The outside software vendor created a secure, web-based software program into which student course histories from multiple institutions are uploaded and which serves as a central solution for audit prior to official transcript exchanges between specific institutions. In particular, the final reverse transfer solution was designed to deliver

- seamless access and user-friendly interfaces at all public and private institutions in the state,

- the ability to integrate electronic transcripts from multiple student information systems,

- the ability to run large numbers of automated degree audits against preloaded degree pathways, and

- the ability to extract course- and credit-level aggregate data and reports for enhancement and research purposes.

The degree-audit solution was also linked to the Tennessee Longitudinal Data System (TLDS), a state Department of Education initiative that tracks student progress from P-16 into the workforce. This link added student and graduate tracking within educational pathways and into the workforce for future research.

Implementation

Following policy refinement and the development of a web-based solution to carry out the functions of reverse transfer came the critical partnerships with institutions and their students. The project first reached out to three pairs of two- and four-year institutions, including one private institution, to pilot the steps of the software solution. A small number of students at each institution agreed to allow their student information and academic histories to be used solely for testing purposes. In the next semester, about half of the state's public institutions participated in the first reverse transfer cycle. Communication with institutional registrars and student information specialists was conducted via webinars. Within TBR and UT systems, information technologists shared the Student Information Systems (SIS) technical scripts required to identify and upload student information. The project coordinator and community college liaison also visited as many institutions as possible and still do so on an annual basis—a challenge in a state that is more than

600 miles long. Onboarding half of the state's public institutions first was wise, and perhaps still too ambitious in retrospect. In the second cycle, all public institutions, as well as a few private institutions, participated in the program.

Reaching Students

Finally, communication and messaging to students were essential for program success. Key issues included convincing students to (a) open an email and recognize reverse transfer as a real opportunity with no cost, (b) consent to release transcripts for degree evaluation, and (c) recognize the value of earning an associate degree. The marketing and communication workgroup from the Reverse Transfer Task Force, as well as the in-house communications teams at UT and TBR, partnered to create multiple methods for effective student communication. Planning included FERPA-compliant content for student consent messages, number and timing of emails to potentially eligible students, and methods for keeping campus advisors and registrars informed about and involved in reverse transfer system enhancements. Additionally, broad marketing plans were created for the state and institutions to implement. Strategies included billboards, posters, postcards, orientation messages, emails, and phone calls. Although the program relied heavily on marketing at four-year institutions where eligible students were enrolled, both four- and two-year institutions played an important role in communications with students.

Outcomes and Impact

Reverse transfer matching and evaluation of student credits occurs twice yearly. Outcomes are posted within the reverse transfer solution and reported to the participating institutions, the Reverse Transfer Task Force, and the Articulation and Transfer Council. Similarly, results are often shared with professional organizations at state and national levels.

The Tennessee formula funding model splits credit for the award between the student's prior community college and current university attended. The credit formula symbolizes the contribution of both institutions to the student's progress and credential. The financial implication is relatively small but important to maintaining the efforts of all the public institutions in the reverse transfer program.

The number of potentially eligible students typically ranges from 6,000 to 8,000 per semester. Using the current process, only about a quarter of those students opt in for further review (see Table 2.1). Data definitions for program reports include the following:

- *number of eligible students:* those identified by four-year institution who have 15 hours of prior community college credit and at least 60 cumulative credit hours;

- *number of opted-in students:* those who received an invitation email from their current four-year school and provided consent and contact information for the sharing of transcripts needed to conduct a formal degree audit by the community college of previous attendance;

- *audit-eligible students:* those who, as identified by the current four-year institution, meet community college GPA and credit hour requirements, as well as total credit hour requirements;

- *number of opted-out students:* students who gave "no response" to the invitation email, who chose to opt out by clicking a link in the invitation email, or who were audit-ineligible;[5]

- *number of degrees awarded:* reverse transfer associate degrees awarded by the community college; and

- *number of degrees not awarded:* number of opted-in students who did not meet degree requirements for an associate degree award.

Table 2.1
Reverse Transfer Outcomes

Cycle	Eligible students	Opt-in	Opt-out by student	Opt-out no response	Degrees awarded
Spring 2015	5,860	1,159 (20%)	39 (1%)	4,662 (80%)	347
Fall 2015	7,514	1,756 (23%)	57 (1%)	5,701 (76%)	460
Spring 2016	8,160	1,533 (19%)	1,453 (18%)[a]	5,174 (63%)	370
Fall 2016	6,173	1,390 (23%)	37 (1%)	4,746 (77%)	317
Totals	**27,707**	**5,838 (21%)**	**1,586 (5%)**	**20,283 (74%)**	**1,267**

[a]For this cycle only, the opt-out total includes both opted-out students and students who already had received associate degrees. A technical error prevented distinction between the two.

Challenges and Solutions

Strengthening partnerships requires a little flexibility and a lot of listening. Continuous feedback is solicited and collected from records personnel and academic administrators; this feedback has driven many improvements to the overall

---

[5] The number of opted-out students is large (typically around 80% of eligible students).

program. Enhancements to the solution interface that save time for community college personnel are prioritized. Timelines and deadlines for data uploads and audits of transcripts are designed around academic calendars; key student information is highlighted to ease screening by graduation specialists. Future goals include improving the screening audit to speed award decisions.

Turnover of institutional contacts is an ongoing challenge; project leads, user roles and institutional technical contacts change frequently. The statewide coordinator regularly reaches out to institutions for updates, but new personnel are still sometimes caught off guard when a reverse transfer cycle begins. Just-in-time training tools and shared documents for maintaining updated user roles are being prepared. The value of an effective and well-known community college liaison cannot be overstated, and the Tennessee team is lucky to have a former longstanding registrar to facilitate connections and outreach to the 13 two-year institutions in the state.

Policy Barriers

Having key policy decisions in place before starting the statewide reverse transfer program eased development and implementation. The large task force ensured that policy issues were readily illuminated and adjusted. THEC policy requires an exit exam measuring students' mastery of general education prior to receiving a degree; a special waiver was granted to allow reverse transfer students to complete the exit exam at the point of baccalaureate graduation. Likewise, transcript and graduation fees were waived to encourage student participation. The reverse transfer policy also allows some course substitutions, although conflicting policy still exists regarding substitutions within the parallel Tennessee Transfer Pathways. Catalog expiration dates are problematic in some instances; at least two community colleges will not consider a reverse transfer degree award if the student's academic career began five or more years prior. TBR affirmed each community college's right to set catalog limits and maintain any other institution-specific graduation requirements.

One of the most contentious issues was determining how to apply credit for a reverse transfer award to the state outcomes formula for funding decisions. Because multiple institutions contribute to a reverse transfer degree, various methods were considered for splitting the formula based on credits earned. Ultimately, the task force and Articulation and Transfer Council recommended an even split for simplicity.

Policy barriers continue to arise in individual cases. Institutions are naturally reluctant to make exceptions that would not be made for native students. The community college system is willing to continue wrestling with these points even as the environment becomes more complex. In 2017, six public universities formerly in the TBR system became independent, locally governed institutions. The higher education commission and the governor have indicated that maintaining progress for transfer is still a high priority; the established intrasystem partnerships will allow the programs to weather these organizational changes, although more individual contact with the six public universities will be necessary.

Student Engagement

Optimizing reverse transfer requires an effective method for obtaining consent. Efforts to increase student engagement have centered on visible marketing efforts to encourage opt-in; however, response to the invitation emails has been low. Tennessee is in the process of implementing alternative opt-in methods, including an opt-in option on community college or four-year transfer applications. Because both two- and four-year institutions are invested in the reverse program, collaboration has increased to provide proactive approaches for students who indicate early on that a four-year degree is their goal. An unanticipated consequence of reverse transfer has been increased attention to dual admissions programs and early advising programs for potential transfer students.

Moving Forward

The reverse transfer initiative created positive momentum in a number of other areas for Tennessee higher education. Those developments are outlined briefly in this section.

Forward Transfer Tools

Lessons learned during the reverse transfer initiative proved valuable as the project turned to supporting forward transfer in the state. Another high-profile initiative, Tennessee Reconnect, began in 2016 to focus on returning adults in colleges and universities. Adult learners and college near-completers are essential to meeting the goals of Drive to 55 and Tennessee's future labor and workforce needs. The tools needed to help adults determine how credits would transfer and apply to a degree were based on the same underlying data and assumptions of the reverse transfer solution. Course inventories, equivalencies, and community college degree requirements were already part of the solution and could be used for both purposes. The team and the statewide partners needed to build out the university degree requirements were already in place. A public online portal and one-stop shop with transfer and degree check tools was launched in early 2016 and has reached more than 100,000 unique users to date.

Course and Content Alignment

Prior to the reverse transfer program, course-level data were held by individual institutions or systems in Tennessee. Reverse transfer cycle data provided the first glimpse into course data and course-taking patterns on a statewide basis. Using a partnership with the Boyd Center for Business and Economic Research, research has begun on the demographic, programmatic, and course-level factors that impact reverse transfer award eligibility. For example, a review of the first few cycles of awards revealed differences in award and course completion by race and Pell Grant eligibility. Further research at the course level will inform advising and transfer patterns and pinpoint areas for detailed work on course sequences and learning outcomes. Long-term research questions in Tennessee include the impact of reverse transfer awards on completion, time to degree, and workforce implications such as employability and earnings.

Future Goals

The team will use research and collective insights to keep moving toward the goal of seamless transfer in Tennessee. The team is optimistic that efforts to increase opt-in numbers will positively correlate with associate degrees earned. Efforts are underway to track the transfer population more effectively and improve progress through course alignment and advising, with emphasis on institutions, regions of the state, and underrepresented student populations for which efforts should be intensified.

Recommendations for Practice

The work around transfer and degree completion in Tennessee may be instructive to other states seeking strategies for increasing access to and successful completion of postsecondary credentials. Specific recommendations drawn from our experience are presented in this section.

Timing Is Important

When building partnerships, initiative fatigue is an element of timing that must be considered. At the time of the state's initial interest in reverse transfer, the higher education systems were heavily engaged in developing transfer paths and in other college completion projects, so many players were skeptical of another major initiative. On the other hand, the working groups and relationships were in place, the UT system had the capacity to lead the project, and the state's political climate was supportive. Pushing through the fatigue actually supported the reverse transfer project.

The timing of policy development was fortuitous as well, as planning and policy development began before funding was secure. With the big-picture decisions already in place, Tennessee was more competitive for funding opportunities and could move to implementation quickly. In building capacity for large initiatives, transfer and reverse transfer advocates may consider whether the need has been recognized in the state, region, or nationally. Data regarding current transfer challenges and opportunities aid the push for policy change. Knowing the biggest gaps and barriers ahead of time allows for preventive planning. With the most crucial problems attacked proactively, teams are ready to proceed when the timing is right.

Use Inclusive Planning, Make Policy Decisions Early

When planning a transfer project including data collection, timelines, marketing, and other considerations, the expertise of the entire project team and others who interface with student information systems is crucial. Higher education is a highly specialized field. With multiple specialists and unit representatives (including students) at the table, knowledge and creativity explode. Presidents, chancellors, and student life personnel can become vocal allies and advocates.

The single most important ingredient for success in Tennessee has been the inclusivity of the Reverse Transfer Task Force, a practice also endorsed by Friedel and Wilson (2015). Carefully selected to bring together information technology, institutional research, policy, and academic representatives from all three higher education systems, the task force has remained a steadfast planning group since the project's inception. The first refresh of the task force has only just occurred, almost five years since the initial gatherings.

Identify and Support a Champion (or Two)

In addition to the inclusive task force, a primary coordinator was appointed, with the reverse transfer project as her sole priority. Available funding ensured the project director could travel across the state and to key conferences as a participant or presenter. The excitement generated by the Credit When It's Due initiative, conversations with other state leaders, and other professional development activities devoted to reverse transfer helped the director act as a true believer and confident cheerleader.

No less critical was the selection of a community college liaison from the companion two-year college system. The wise choice to engage a senior registrar, with connections and credibility across the state, proved essential to understanding the technical details of community college awards to the perspectives and philosophies of all the partners involved.

Use Expert Technical Support

Using a third-party vendor, AcademyOne, created another champion for the Tennessee reverse transfer initiative. Although technical expertise was available in-house, investing in an external developer enlarged the project team and ensured the project was a high priority. The Tennessee team on the ground could focus on policy, process, and implementation and hand over technical development to AcademyOne, which could focus on details an academic group may have missed. Private vendors are also equipped to manage timelines, sequence tasks, and enforce project benchmarks.

Despite working with a team spread across the state and a remote vendor, weekly phone conferences kept the project on schedule. The lead partners at AcademyOne have been integral members of our team and equal partners in its success. The company continues to handle enhancements for the reverse transfer solution while slowly turning over technical management.

That said, development partners must be willing to listen and adapt to higher education norms and expectations, particularly in language and format. The biggest barrier to reverse transfer's effectiveness, for example, has been students' failure to opt in by responding to an email. Recognizing the habits of students, who avoid regular email contact, may have helped us change the opt-in (consent) strategy earlier in development. Additionally, for academic staff, the earliest revisions to the reverse transfer solution interface were made to match the look and navigation of an academic transcript. Other adaptations were necessary to improve speed and ease of reviewing student histories.

Communicate Regularly, Listen to End Users

One of the best decisions made for Tennessee Reverse Transfer was embarking on a road trip of the state. Over a few weeks each year, the project director, community college liaison, and others visit as many campuses as possible. These visits allow for open discussions with administrators and staff who use the reverse transfer solution. In-person meetings opened up dialogue regarding campus experiences. Conversations during these visits provided clarity on policy and procedure and produced suggestions for future enhancements. Frequently, concerns about other academic issues arose as well and could be passed on to the appropriate unit or individual. No virtual method can replace the value of extended face-to-face discussion.

Review and Improve Continuously

The state tour was one of many examples of efforts to review and improve the reverse transfer program. Most recently, the statewide Transfer Summit included a session for each type of campus partner (i.e., admissions and registrars, records, adult learner contacts) to share experiences and come up with a new wish list. Feedback notes are kept by the project director but could be housed in a central document accessible to the whole team for reference. Enhancements based on feedback are reported during each annual task force meeting and through occasional electronic messages, closing the loop with end-users and affirming their concerns are heard. With this approach, the project is never considered finished, keeping the focus on continual improvement and expansion.

Celebrate Accomplishments

People, relationships, and partnerships drive student success in higher education. Recognizing and celebrating accomplishments with colleagues before moving to the next task is critical to maintaining momentum and program excellence. Celebrations, as simple as silly emails or as elaborate as conference presentations and awards, acknowledge teamwork and common purpose. Notes and small gifts, such as restaurant gift cards, are kind gestures to recognize individual work. The positive energy of celebration fosters team renewal so the group is ready to tackle next steps and move forward. Efforts in building, nurturing, and celebrating partnerships lay a strong foundation for transfer initiatives.

Conclusion

The legislative climate, higher education system relationships, and partnerships with private foundations and industry all contributed to the launch of Tennessee Reverse Transfer and Tennessee Reconnect initiatives. The loss of any one of these elements would have delayed or sidelined these initiatives. Prospects were daunting at first, but large, representative advisory groups and a smaller team of dedicated personnel enabled the initiatives' success. Constant communication, enhancements based on user feedback, and occasional celebrations fostered lasting ownership among all the stakeholders and participants.

References

Complete College Tennessee Act of 2010, Tenn. Code Ann. § 49-7-202 (2010). Retrieved from Justia U.S. Law website https://law.justia.com/codes/tennessee/2010/title-49/chapter-7/part-2/49-7-202/

Friedel, J. N., & Wilson, S. L. (2015). The new reverse transfer: A national landscape. *Community College Journal of Research and Practice, 39*(1), 70-86.

Garcia, S. A. (2015, March). *Reverse transfer: The national landscape* (CWID Data Note No. 1). Champaign, IL: Office of Community College Research and Leadership, University of Illinois at Urbana-Champaign.

Lumina Foundation. (2017). *A stronger nation 2017.* Retrieved from http://strongernation.luminafoundation.org/report/2017/#nation

Taylor, J. L. (2016). Reverse credit transfer policies and programs: Policy rationales, implementation, and implications. *Community College Journal of Research and Practice, 40*(12), 1074-1090.

Taylor, J. L., & Bragg, D. D. (2015, January). *Optimizing reverse transfer policies and processes: Lessons from twelve CWID states.* Champaign, IL: Office of Community College Research and Leadership. University of Illinois at Urbana-Champaign.

Tennessee Higher Education Commission (THEC). (2017). *Articulation and transfer in Tennessee higher education 2016-2017.* Retrieved from https://www.tn.gov/content/dam/tn/thec/bureau/research/other-research/all-other/articulation/Articulation_Transfer_Report_2017_Final.pdf

Townsend, B., & Dever, J. (1999). What do we know about reverse transfer students? In B. K. Townsend (Ed.), *Understanding the impact of reverse transfer students on community colleges* (New Directions for Community Colleges No. 106, pp. 5-14). San Francisco, CA: Jossey Bass.

CHAPTER **3**

TRANSFER READINESS: INSIGHTS FROM **10 YEARS** OF **INTENTIONAL DESIGN**

Joyce C. Romano and Maria L. Hesse

Over the past 10 years we have had the opportunity to work intentionally on designing transfer pathways for students in our respective states, Florida and Arizona. The work has required large-scale implementation within diverse and complex educational institutions involving tens of thousands of students. The goal has been to increase the number of students who are transferring from community colleges to universities, prepared for success in their desired majors, and completing their associate and bachelor's degrees, while reducing time and costs to degree completion.

Both the DirectConnect to UCF program, between Valencia College and the University of Central Florida, and the Maricopa to ASU Pathways Program, between the Maricopa Community Colleges and Arizona State University, have focused heavily on the strategy of defining pathways, which is also the recent focus of national initiatives (e.g., the American Association of Community Colleges Pathways Project, Completion by Design, Complete College America). While definitions differ (Salaman, 2016), this work usually includes identifying the specific courses required during the first 60 credits of a particular bachelor's degree so that students complete their associate degree and enter the university in their junior year. This way, they are on track to complete a bachelor's degree within the next 60 credits. Some initiatives sequence the course plans term by term, and some recommend specific courses that are traditionally identified within programs of study as electives. For example, a specific humanities course might be included instead of listing the choice as "three credits, humanities elective," especially when the specific course satisfies both a general education and a program prerequisite requirement. Pathways may include other features such as communication flows to students, websites with resources, progress milestones, program learning outcomes aligned to workforce or graduate school preparation, and tracking software and notifications to students when they are off track.

Most educators who delve into detailed pathways quickly realize why the choices are confusing to students, particularly community college students, who are more likely to be first-generation college students and have to negotiate their way through not just one, but two institutions. Sorting out common prerequisites, program prerequisites, and recommended versus truly optional electives from the descriptions in college catalogs is a lesson in the real complexity of academic programs. Transfer students are often disappointed when they find that some coursework taken at a community college does not count at the university or did not shorten the time to bachelor's degree completion. Pathways programs are designed to simplify student choices, making the path from associate degree to bachelor's degree more transparent. Pathways assist students and advisors with clarifying the coursework to take at the community college so that the courses both transfer and apply to the specific bachelor's degree program the student aspires to complete at the university.

Pathways are a means to improve student transfer success, but the curricular clarity that defines many pathways programs, while important, is not all that is necessary to make students transfer-ready. After describing two pathways programs, the authors will discuss factors that should be considered by community college and university educators working to prepare students for a successful transition between their institutions, and completion of both their associate and bachelor's degrees.

Model Pathways Programs

The model programs described here provide students with clarity about what coursework to take at their community college so that they can simultaneously complete associate and bachelor's degree requirements. This emphasis on clarity and simplicity was largely inspired by Scott-Clayton's (2011) research on choice among community college students. Drawing on behavioral economics and psychology, she argues that the emphasis on *individual choice* does a disservice to community college students who often make less than optimal decisions. Scott-Clayton advocates for programs that are tightly and consciously structured, with relatively little room to unintentionally deviate from paths toward completion, and with limited bureaucratic obstacles for students to circumnavigate. Similarly, McClenney (2012) suggests incoming community college students be required to follow a structured process for entry, orientation, and ongoing advising and support, noting that "students don't do optional."

DirectConnect to UCF Program

Valencia College in Orlando, Florida, began the DirectConnect to UCF program in 2006 with the University of Central Florida (UCF) and three other area community colleges in order to guarantee local students access to university bachelor's programs. Valencia enrolls more than 70,000 students annually, and

UCF enrolls more than 64,000 students annually. Through DirectConnect to UCF, associate degree graduates are guaranteed admission to UCF and have the same access to limited enrollment bachelor's programs as native (i.e., admitted as first-time, first-year) UCF students. DirectConnect to UCF emphasizes the student experience, a smooth transition from college to university, shared use of facilities, strong academic program alignment, and integrated student services. Admissions and orientation programs are aligned so students can move seamlessly to UCF, and UCF advisors on Valencia campuses help students develop educational plans for a smooth transition. UCF brings its bachelor's programs to Valencia through regional campuses at the community college. Because of this, shared-use facilities such as state-of-the-art classrooms, testing centers, studios, computer labs, and study rooms provide students with access to expanded program offerings, increased flexibility, and lower travel costs.

This seamless web of programs and services has led to increased academic opportunities and achievement for the partner colleges' students at both the associate and baccalaureate levels. Since its inception, DirectConnect to UCF has proven highly productive, fiscally responsible and scalable, and has withstood both the best and worst budget conditions. Its participants now make up a bigger share of new students at UCF than incoming first-year students (39% compared with 36% in 2016-2017). Valencia students (who started at UCF at various times) comprised 24% of all UCF bachelor degree recipients in 2016-2017. More than half (55%) of the bachelor's graduates who started at Valencia College were under-represented minorities, which significantly added to the diversity of the university's student body.

Maricopa to ASU Pathways Program

Built as an extension of Arizona State University's (ASU) highly successful eAdvisor program and initially funded by a $1 million grant from the Kresge Foundation, the Maricopa to ASU Pathways Program (MAPP) is another national model for helping community college students understand requirements and receive continuous support in order to prepare for success at ASU. The Maricopa Community Colleges, located in the metropolitan Phoenix area, enroll about 200,000 students per year; approximately 40% of those students indicate a desire to eventually transfer and earn a bachelor's degree. Annually, more than 5,500 new transfer students from the Maricopa Community Colleges enroll at ASU, about half of whom are part of the MAPP, which was initially implemented in Fall 2009.

Students in MAPP are guaranteed admission to the specific degree and major at the university to which they aspire. The pathways build in the appropriate Arizona General Education Curriculum (AGEC) and a full transfer associate degree.

Thus, students who enter the university come as true juniors and have a maximum of 60 credits remaining for graduation. Credits on a pathway transfer and apply to a student's designated major, providing a cost-effective and time-efficient plan for students. ASU's critical tracking course requirements are built into each pathway so that community college students take courses equivalent to those of their university peers, paralleling as much as possible the curriculum of the university's major map (i.e., ASU's terminology for a sequenced curricular plan to degree completion). Critical tracking courses help a student determine whether they are an appropriate fit for a given major. The language of the community college identifies courses on the pathways; that is, the community college course numbers and titles are used so students and advisors do not have to reference other documents (e.g., college catalogs).

The pledge to students is "no surprises." Any special requirements are printed on pathway documents so that requirements for a specific major are clearly identified in advance. For example, if a given major requires a higher GPA for admission or anything the student or advisor should be aware of, it is easily seen on the document.

As we continue to perfect the design and execution of pathways programs, more than 10 years of work and experience have revealed that defined curricular plans are a foundational but not sufficient condition for transfer readiness. To help transfer students succeed in both their transition to university and eventual completion of a bachelor's degree, they need to be prompted to reflect on a number of topics we believe will help them become ready for success. After working with faculty, advisors, and students on transfer systems, looking at data on transfer patterns, listening to feedback, and considering our students' experience, we suggest a more comprehensive model for transfer readiness. This model includes several dimensions, one of them being curricular clarity. Our working theory is that true educational access requires students to be prepared across several dimensions in order to be truly transfer-ready.

In the remaining sections of this chapter, we will describe components of transfer readiness, discuss why they are important, including relevant research that we identified, and suggest ways that students can be engaged in their personal development within the dimension.

Transfer Readiness Model

We suggest six dimensions for transfer readiness that together address the comprehensive way students can prepare for bachelor's degree completion, in particular for students who earn their bachelor's degree by starting with an associate degree. Traditionally, this means completing the first 60 credits at a community college and the second 60 credits at a university, but these dimensions could also be relevant to students who use other combinations of credits or other combinations of higher education institutions to reach bachelor's completion. In fact, recent research on a national sample of transfer students found that 8.1% of students actually complete the bachelor's following the 2+2 model, while the most common (19.9%) pattern was enrollment with breaks (Jenkins & Fink, 2016). Because the 2+2 terminology may imply to students that they can expect to finish their associate degree in two years and their bachelor's degree in another two years, and research shows this does not happen often, the authors have coined another term that might help briefly describe the associate to bachelor's path: A2B.

We contend that if community college and university educators are to help students successfully transition between institutions while completing both their associate and bachelor's degrees, students should be encouraged to reflect upon, and institutional practices should be designed around, six dimensions of transfer readiness.

- *Personal aspirations*—"People like me can ... " A belief that students from their own background can be successful, belong, and are welcomed into higher education in general and an aspirational profession (e.g., engineer, doctor, teacher, nurse, scientist) in particular.

- *Purpose*—Students clarify their personal direction and goals and can tie their career aspirations to a set of educational programs that can move them in that direction, even if those goals emerge and change over time.

- *Curricular plan*—Students complete course prerequisites for specific bachelor's programs with few excess credits so that all (or most) lower-division coursework satisfies the requirements for a bachelor's degree and permits direct entry into upper-division coursework.

- *Academic preparation*—Students demonstrate ability to achieve in the specific academic discipline they are pursuing, including the ability to demonstrate academic rigor, knowing how to persist when the academic work is challenging, and the expectations for learning (learning how to learn) in that discipline.

- *Career preparation*—Students understand the expectations for professional behavior in the career field. This may include learning through undergraduate research, internships, and academic mentors. It includes gaining an understanding of what is involved in the day-to-day life of the chosen profession and committing to the life that it entails.

- *Social preparation*—Students understand and adopt behavioral expectations for success at the university. This includes physical and behavioral navigation, an emphasis on independence, the ability to self-advocate, and the ability to plan financially as well as academically for degree completion.

Personal Aspirations

It is in the fabric of the United States to believe that anyone can be anything they want. Despite Americans' foundational belief in all possibilities and stirring individual examples of accomplishment, the data still show that socioeconomic background factors are significantly correlated with academic success and bachelor's degree completion. A longitudinal study of high school students by the National Center for Education Statistics (NCES, 2014) showed that only 14% of students from low socioeconomic backgrounds had completed a bachelor's degree, compared with 60% of students from high socioeconomic status.

Two theories provide insight into the conditions that shape students' personal aspirations: neighborhood resource theory and collective socialization theory (Gandara, 2002). With respect to neighborhood resource theory, the quality of local resources available to families, as well as the ability of parents to use them, affects child development outcomes. Collective socialization theory suggests that more affluent neighborhoods generally provide more successful role models and stronger normative support for the kinds of behavior associated with school success. Thus, the availability of resources and access to role models may have an impact on whether students see themselves as college material and the types of jobs they see themselves performing in the future.

Similarly, Adelman (2002) found that *anticipations* or "the level and consistency of a student's vision of his/her future education" (p. 50) was second only to academic preparation in predicting bachelor's degree completion. These two factors were strong enough to reinforce each other in all three communities studied—urban, suburban, and rural or small town (Adelman, 2002).

Students often start at community college with vague notions of career possibilities, or with specific aspirations and little knowledge of what it takes academically or otherwise to reach those career goals. For example, more than 3,000 enrolled students at Valencia have indicated they are pre-nursing; however, the program only admits 225 students a year, and many who indicate this interest do not achieve the entry requirements. Similarly, STEM fields have been emphasized in high school and college as a good major choice because of job availability and high salaries, leading many students to indicate interest in engineering at college entry. Many do so, however, without much understanding of the different fields within engineering or without a realistic assessment of their interest or ability to complete calculus and physics course requirements.

Career discovery and choice is part of the career development process that is expected during college student development (Gordon & Sears, 1997). However, it seems that students are being asked to make career decisions at a younger age, often during the middle or high school years. Most bachelor's degrees have specific requirements, and the requirements for a finance major are different from those for an electrical engineering or Spanish major. So community college students who are undecided about their career direction may not know what college major to declare and therefore may take coursework that is not relevant to the bachelor's degree they eventually decide to pursue.

Higher education is a goal, or at least a hope, across most communities and socioeconomic levels in the United States. Yet, the actual possibilities involved and the decisions that need to be made in a timely way to turn those possibilities into reality are not well known across all communities. This results in limited options for many Americans. Transferring to a university may be a goal for a larger number of community college students, but many struggle to get on the right curricular pathway until they have had the opportunity to better understand career options. For students from some backgrounds, the known choices for careers are often limited to what they see "someone like them" doing. All colleges and universities must make opportunities for early assessments of and ongoing reflections about aspirations and career interests available to their students.

In *Hillbilly Elegy,* J. D. Vance (2016) shares his life journey from a background of poverty and dysfunction in Appalachia to Yale Law School, basing his career choice on what he saw "the rich kids" doing: They "were born either doctors or lawyers and I didn't want to work with blood" (p. 181). Vance has had an exceptional life, yet one wonders what other options he might have considered had he been presented opportunities for assessing his interests and skills, learning about career options, shadowing professionals in potential areas of interest, and reflecting on these exposures in light of his personal interests and aspirations.

College preparation programs for disadvantaged youth (e.g., TRIO, GEAR UP) usually have a strong component that exposes participants to career choice by introducing role models from similar backgrounds, promoting career exploration programs and college visits, and encouraging students to identify their interests and talents as they consider their future (Swail & Perna, 2002). The challenge is how to embed this deep level of exposure and possibility for every student of every age when they enter college.

In 2015, ASU developed a free, interactive career tool that helps connect college majors with career interests. The *me3* tool, which started as a web-based implement, is now available for use on smartphones. As of Fall 2017, me3 had been used by more than 100,000 high school and college students (Ell, 2017). As students make choices as part of a visual quiz, the tool calculates their RIASEC (realistic, investigative, artistic, social, enterprising, conventional) score, which represents their level of interest in data, things, people, and ideas. Then me3 compares their scores to those of more than 500 careers based on data provided by the U.S. Department of Labor. Students see careers with scores most similar to their individual results and then learn about college majors that can help them prepare for those career options.

In 2014, Valencia College added the New Student Experience Course as a requirement for all new degree-seeking students. The course includes six learning outcomes along the dimensions of Purpose, Pathway, Plan, Preparation, Place, and Personal Connection. Many colleges offer similar courses as required or optional. A college entry culture that expects and supports personal exploration combined with realistic planning will encourage students to accomplish goals they may not have previously considered.

Purpose

Defining one's purpose allows an individual to achieve fulfillment in life. When students express frustration that their life is going nowhere, it is often a sign that they have not fully reflected on their purpose. Executive coach and author of *The Power of Purpose*, Richard Leider (2008) explains, "Purpose is the conscious choice of what, where, and how to make a positive contribution in our world. It is the theme, quality, or passion we choose to center our lives around" (p. 28).

Leider contends that people who understand what motivates them, what defines them as a person, and what they want out of life, are apt to be happier, healthier, and more fulfilled. Purpose can be seen as the reason someone works to achieve a goal. Students who know who they are and what they want from their lives are positioned to make better decisions about their future. And once students begin to understand what direction they are heading, it is easier to select majors or programs of study and pursue other activities in college that will help them move toward their goals. Some students will know what career they want to pursue; thus, an advisor can share information about a set of majors that will lead them in the direction of that career. Others may only know careers they decidedly do not want to pursue. Some students have a sense of broad areas they enjoy, but are unfamiliar with all the options within those clusters.

Cuseo (2005) grapples with the challenges faced by students who are undecided about their college major and the implications for academic advising, career counseling, and student retention. He contends that educators should not confuse a student's inability to declare a major with a lack of commitment. Cuseo provides examples of students with multiple interests, those with a thorough and deliberate decision-making style, and others who may not feel comfortable making career declarations and therefore selecting a major upon college entry. He suggests that for some students, "exploratory" or "investigative" might be a more accurate label. He adds that

> The fact that such large numbers of students change their initially cho-sen major—coupled with research findings indicating that students who change majors are as likely, or more likely, to attain good grades and persist to graduation—serve to support institutional policies that encourage students to postpone initial decisions about an academic major until they gain more self-knowledge and more personal experi-ence with the college curriculum. (Cuseo, 2005, p. 6)

Cuseo (2005) concludes that strategies for enhancing the quality of a first-year student's experience include meeting regularly with a seasoned and committed advisor for conversations about who they want to become as a person, what they are interested in, and making wise choices about course-taking; promoting courses that help students reflect on their future goals and aspirations; front-loading exposure to career services; offering special resources for students who are still exploring careers and majors; and creating experiential learning opportunities that make them aware of the realities of work in different careers.

From the perspective of building pathways for transfer students, these issues support the need for developing *meta-majors*, or sets of courses that meet the academic requirements across several related disciplines and programs of study. At Valencia College, students can select from one of eight meta-majors to guide course choice and advising assignments: (a) arts, humanities, communication, and design; (b) business; (c) education; (d) health sciences; (e) industry/manufactur-ing and construction; (f) public safety; (g) STEM; and (h) social and behavioral sciences and human services. New students to ASU who are undecided on a major are required to enter as an "exploratory student" in one of seven meta-majors or tracks: (a) social and behavioral sciences; (b) humanities, fine arts, and design; (c) math, physical sciences, engineering, and technology; (d) applied computing, mathematics, and technology; (e) health and life sciences; (f) business; and (g) education. Administrators and faculty believe that exploratory status does not limit students' choices; rather, it enables students to begin meeting general education requirements while taking a variety of academic courses that may spark interest in a specific career and major.

The broader point here is that students who are able to identify their purpose—their reason for being—are more likely to be prepared for career exploration and the associated academic preparation.

Curricular Plan

As noted earlier, much national attention over the past several years has been given to creating specific associate to bachelor's degree (A2B) pathways and getting students on track to follow them. Three national pathways initiatives focused on community colleges exemplify this focus. We also identify other resources and ideas relevant to developing coherent curricular plans for students.

The American Association of Community Colleges (2015) Pathways Project is an integrated, institution-wide approach that advocates for clarifying paths to student end goals through creating program maps and transfer pathways; helping students choose and enter a pathway; providing strong advising and using of appropriate technology tools and other resources to keep students on the path; and ensuring that students learn through effective teaching practices and assessment of program learning outcomes.

Completion by Design was a major Gates Foundation-funded community college reform designed to increase the proportion of low-income and first-generation students who earn college degrees while shortening their time to degree completion. Participating colleges aligned policies, programs, and practices to create guided pathways to better support students. They defined a guided pathway as a "clear and coherent map that integrates academic and support services across the student experience" (Achieving the Dream, 2016a). They also compiled a toolkit (Achieving the Dream, 2016b) to help other institutions understand the rationale for the project, assess their readiness for undertaking a guided pathways initiative, and learn from the successes and challenges of other colleges.

Complete College America (2018) makes the case that too many barriers to college student success exist, including low credit enrollment; poorly designed and delivered remedial education; overwhelming and unclear choices; and unresponsive higher education systems. This organization encourages embedding remediation in corequisite courses; establishing a new norm of 15-credit hour enrollment each term; providing alternative math pathways; providing structured schedules; and establishing degree plans instead of individual course enrollment in order to accelerate degree completion.

Tracking Transfer (Jenkins & Fink, 2016) is a recent study by the Community College Research Center from which the Transfer Playbook was derived.

It includes four recommended strategies to strengthen bachelor's completion: (a) prioritize transfer success, (b) create clear program pathways with aligned high-quality instruction, (c) provide tailored transfer student advising, and (d) build strong transfer partnerships (Wyner, Deane, Jenkins, & Fink, 2016).

Many colleges are implementing or considering software programs that track student progression along a specific curricular plan and alert students and advisors when a student's course enrollment does not match the specified plan. Some of these systems have additional alerts for students and advisors when a student takes an action deemed as high-risk to program progression or completion, so that college staff can intervene or provide guidance to get the student back on track.

In conversations and structured focus groups, students regularly say they want to make sure not to waste their time by taking courses they do not need. Clear curricular plans clarify the path for students who are interested in knowing exactly what to do and when during their time at a community college to ensure their work will "count" at the university. It has also been our experience that having a curricular plan laid out in advance, and using tracking software and pathway audit tools, saves advisors time, allowing them to have more important conversations with students about purpose, life goals, career interests, and preparation for a fulfilling future.

Valencia College developed and implemented its LifeMap program, which includes online planning tools for students to create and save their career and educational plans, in 1999. LifeMap is a progression stage model that starts with College Transition when students are still in high school and continues to Graduation Transition. It guides students on "what to do when" through programs, online resources, and conversations with advisors and faculty in a holistic system. Since 2015, Valencia has added assigned program advisors based on a student's meta-major so that each student can have a continued relationship with an advisor who is an expert in the particular program of study. This is part of the comprehensive Student Success Pathway that Valencia is implementing and includes the New Student Experience program (described elsewhere in the chapter).

The ASU MAPP is part of the university's eAdvisor system, designed to assist students with personalized, on-demand tools to guide and support them toward success in their college journey. While at the community college, MAPP students can access several ASU tools. The Degree Search tool helps students learn more about various majors and the careers associated with them. The student's MyASU account is a personal portal with links to the student's transfer specialist and academic advisor; a calendar of important dates for transfer students; financial resources; and more.

As many transfers will have earned credits at multiple colleges and universities, one key to helping them develop a comprehensive educational plan is knowing how the university will count previous coursework; the Transfer Credit Guide lets students see how courses taken at their current community college or elsewhere will count at ASU. The Pathway Progress Tracker tool allows a student from one of the Maricopa Community Colleges to view a pathway audit showing courses that have been completed, are in progress, or remain to be completed, pertinent to the specific university major the student aspires to achieve. Note that Maricopa advisors and other student affairs and academic affairs staff can also access these ASU tools for their prospective transfer students.

Academic Preparation

Curriculum development assumes that entry courses are building blocks of knowledge that prepare students for subsequent higher level courses in the academic program. Course grades are assumed to indicate a student's demonstrated mastery of the course content, and minimum grades (e.g., C or better) or a minimum GPA is often required to continue in a course sequence to earn an associate degree. It is assumed that success in a prerequisite course will lead to success in subsequent courses in the sequence. Course-level success data shared between UCF and Valencia College showed that in selective STEM-related courses, students who completed the prerequisite with a B or better passed the higher level course at rates of 70-84%, while those with a C or lower passed the course at rates of 60% (UCF: IKM, 2016).

The achievement of course grades, however, also reflects the student's ability to demonstrate mastery in the structure of the course, as well as the expectations of the faculty member, the mode of assessment used to demonstrate learning, the academic and social-emotional supports available and used as needed, and the student's resilience to persevere when struggling with course content. These are critical academic behaviors learned during the associate degree program that must then be applied at the bachelor's degree level in a new academic environment. Tinto (2012) asserts that students are more likely to succeed in college in settings that establish clear and high expectations for their success, provide academic and social support, offer frequent assessment and feedback about their learning, and engage them with others.

The necessary academic behaviors are also specific to the academic discipline the student is pursuing. Part of the academic development that occurs during courses at the associate degree level involves gaining insight and understanding about how to approach the discipline itself, whether that is biology, engineering, psychology, or the humanities. It is a way of thinking about and viewing the world that is specific to the discipline. It is the vocabulary and the shortcuts to knowing and doing embedded in every discipline. This is part of the intentional learning transfer students will need to bring with them to the university in order to make connections with the discipline and faculty at the university level.

In a review of college interventions for economically disadvantaged students, Gandara (2002) found academic weaknesses were addressed through summer bridge programs, tutors, and peer study groups, and these interventions were effective when aligned with a rigorous curriculum and guided by an expert leader. The challenge is to embed strategies across the learning experience so all students can benefit from this level of intentional learning and preparation. Faculty have a critical role in this learning, as they have knowledge of the discipline and can structure courses to include learning about the expectations and customs within the discipline in addition to specific course content. Discipline-based discussions across associate and bachelor's degree faculty groups can add to the alignment of student learning outcomes that include learning discipline-related expectations.

Career Preparation

Career development theory outlines a process of discovery that includes self-assessment, understanding careers, and choosing an educational path toward a certain career or career field (Gordon & Sears, 1997). The process is an iterative one in which learning in one area informs development in the others, and each area may be re-examined after continued discovery and trial of initial decisions.

Many students who start their postsecondary education in a community college have vague notions about their talents or interests, career possibilities, and recommended educational paths for specific careers. So learning outcomes for the associate degree must include learning about career options, educational pathways to those options, and additional learning experiences expected in order to succeed in the career.

An example is undergraduate research, which is increasingly required for entry into limited-access bachelor's programs as well as preparation for graduate education. Some universities require junior-level status to enter into internships in specific disciplines, but without prior experience preparing for undergraduate research in the first or second year, it is very difficult for new transfer students to be ready or competitive for junior-level undergraduate research experiences. Increasingly, colleges offer forms of undergraduate research as part of the associate degree experience, introducing students to the methodology and expectations for developing proposals, conducting research, and sharing results publicly.

Internships and job shadowing are additional ways associate degree students can obtain real-world experience and test their career interests. Many students are attracted to business majors but may not have a good understanding of the difference between specific careers such as finance, accounting, and economics.

Learning about different job opportunities and career trajectories, meeting professionals in these fields and shadowing them on-site in their work environment, completing internships, and other such opportunities help students clarify their expectations. Students in the Maricopa to ASU Pathways Program have access to ASU's Career and Professional Development Services, which lets them engage in career assessment and identify potential internships and jobs.

Academic mentors, industry speakers, and service-learning are other ways in which colleges introduce students to real-world career opportunities. The intentional design of these kinds of experiences into the curricular and cocurricular program should ensure that these are common experiences for graduates of associate and bachelor's degrees.

Social Preparation

For most transfer students, the university is a bigger and more complex educational institution than they were used to at community college. Even at large community colleges such as Valencia, the student experience feels smaller because they attend a specific campus with a smaller number of buildings and 25–35 students per class. In addition, community colleges are generally simpler organizationally. There is less specialization of offices and staff, and services are generally offered on a smaller scale than at the university.

The social preparation for transfer includes adjusting to the size and complexity of a university as well as expectations for independence and self-direction. Most students who go to community college directly from high school feel that more self-direction is expected in college; a similar magnitude of change occurs when the transfer student arrives at the university. Transfer students need to be prepared to navigate and self-advocate to fully engage the university community.

Part of the community college culture includes reducing barriers, providing assistance, and extending second chances when things do not go right the first time. Grade forgiveness policies offer evidence of cultural differences between community colleges and universities. Transfer students need to be prepared for the differences in academic policies and expectations they will encounter. For example, while Valencia College allows unlimited grade forgiveness for students who want to repeat a course to improve their learning if they have below a C grade, UCF only allows grade forgiveness twice. With intentional alignment, associate degree preparation should provide the guidance students need to prepare for the university learning environment.

Social connection is important for student success at the university, as students who gain connections will benefit from a holistic learning experience and can better locate support and assistance as needed. Also, universities have tremendous resources and services to support students and their learning experiences. The diversity of programs, services, opportunities, and connections is a rich resource that greatly enhances the bachelor's degree experience beyond course enrollment. It is critical to transfer students' overall education that they take the time and energy to invest in these opportunities as a part of their university experience. These students' preparation while at community college should include an interest and readiness to fully immerse into university life. Students in the MAPP program, for example, are encouraged to visit ASU while still enrolled at community college. They are invited to attend university events, and they receive communications with university news to prepare them for what lies ahead. Further, they are encouraged to participate in transfer orientation and welcome-week activities to fully engage in the university experience.

A final aspect of social preparation for transfer students is financial planning to allow for completing a bachelor's degree without interruption in enrollment or taking on debt. At the same time, students who work will need to balance employment and course enrollment successfully to achieve academic success. Financial literacy should start at the community college, if not before, so that the practice and skills associated with financial health are carried forward to bachelor's degree completion and beyond.

Conclusion

In 2009, President Barack Obama announced a goal of 60% of U.S. adults having a postsecondary credential by 2020. At the time, the rate was 41%. In 2016, the rate had increased to 48%, through a great deal of effort and investment from public and private sources (Fry, 2017). Clearly, reaching the 60% goal will require new approaches and strategies.

Since 39% of students in higher education (6.7 million) start their journey to a bachelor's degree at a community college (NCES, 2016), we believe an overall increase in postsecondary degree attainment will require addressing transfer student success. From our experience, we see that individual student achievement and degree completion take a great deal of personal effort and collective support, given the life challenges and complexities that many students face.

Developing curricular pathways is an important element in the overall model; while foundational, they are, in and of themselves, insufficient for transfer student success. Elements for transfer readiness highlight additional considerations for students and institutions and suggest ways to align community college and university systems to prepare and support transfer students.

We are challenged and moved by Malcolm Gladwell's (2008) observation at the end of *Outliers* on the need for comprehensive system redesign:

We are so caught up in the myths of the best and brightest and the self-made that we think that outliers spring naturally from the earth. We look at the young Bill Gates and marvel that our world allowed that 13-year-old to become a fabulously successful entrepreneur. But that's the wrong lesson. Our world only allowed one 13-year-old unlimited access to a time-sharing terminal in 1968. If a million teenagers had been given the same opportunity, how many more Microsofts would we have today? To build a better world we need to replace the patchwork of lucky breaks and arbitrary advantages ... with a society that provides opportunities for all. (p. 268)

The implications for community colleges include a concerted focus on career and academic planning, as well as other forms of student preparation and development. The implications for universities are equally important. Some transfer students have needs that are similar to those of incoming first-year students, but others have varied life and previous college experiences that necessitate more personalized assessment of their transfer readiness and appropriate assistance. The growing transfer student population requires administrators at both types of institutions to provide more comprehensive, coordinated programs and services for transfer student success.

References

Achieving the Dream. (2016a). *Completion by design framework*. Retrieved from http://achievingthedream.org/resource/16122/building-guided-pathways-practical-lessons-from-completion-by-design-colleges

Achieving the Dream. (2016b). *Completion by design toolkit*. Retrieved from http://achievingthedream.org/sites/default/files/resources/building_guided_pathways_toolkit_2_16.pdf

Adelman, C. (2002). The relationship between urbanicity and educational outcomes. In W. G. Tierney & L. S. Hagedorn, *Increasing access to college: Extending possibilities for all students* (pp. 35-63). Albany, NY: State University of New York Press.

American Association of Community Colleges (2015). *Pathways project*. Retrieved from https://www.aacc.nche.edu/programs/aacc-pathways-project/

Complete College America. (2018). *Strategies*. Retrieved from https://complete-college.org/completion-roadmap/

Cuseo, J. (2005). "Decided," "undecided," and "in transition": Implications for academic advisement, career counseling, & student retention. Retrieved from http://bit.ly/2LY5pVw

Ell, J. (2017). ASU career tool me3 reaches 100,000 users, launches smartphone app. Retrieved from https://asunow.asu.edu/20171011-asu-news-career-tool-me3-hits-100K-users-launches-phone-app

Fry, R. (2017, January 18). U.S. still has a ways to go in meeting Obama's goal of producing more college grads. *FactTank*. Retrieved from http://www.pewresearch.org/fact-tank/2017/01/18/u-s-still-has-a-ways-to-go-in-meeting-obamas-goal-of-producing-more-college-grads/

Gandara, P. (2002). Meeting common goals: Linking K12 and college interventions. In W. G. Tierney & L. S. Hagedorn (Eds.), *Increasing access to college: Extending possibilities for all students* (pp. 81-103). Albany, NY: State University of New York Press.

Gladwell, M. (2008). *Outliers: The story of success.* New York, NY: Little, Brown.

Gordon, V., & Sears, S. (1997). *Academic alternatives: Exploration and decision-making.* Upper Saddle River, NJ: Gorsuch Scarisbrick.

Jenkins, D., & Fink, J. (2016, January). *Tracking transfer: New measures of institutional and state effectiveness in helping community college students attain bachelor's degrees.* New York, NY: Community College Resource Center, Teachers College, Columbia University. Retrieved from http://ccrc.tc.columbia.edu/publications/tracking-transfer-institutional-state-effectiveness.html

Leider, R. J. (2008). *The power of purpose: Find meaning, live longer, better.* Oakland, CA: Berrett-Koehler, p. 28.

McClenney, K. (2012). *Center for Community College Engagement. A matter of degrees: Promising practices for community college success (a first look).* Austin, TX: Center for Community College Engagement, The University of Texas at Austin, Community College Leadership Program.

National Center for Education Statistics (NCES). (2014). *Postsecondary attainment: Differences by socioeconomic status.* Washington, DC: U.S. Department of Education. Retrieved from https://nces.ed.gov/programs/coe/pdf/coe_tva.pdf

National Center for Education Statistics (NCES). (2016). *Undergraduate enrollment.* Retrieved from https://nces.ed.gov/programs/coe/indicator_cha.asp

Salaman, M. (2016). *Bringing guided pathways to life: 25 strategies for community college leaders and innovators.* Washington, DC: Educational Advisory Board.

Scott-Clayton, J. (2011). *The shapeless river: Does a lack of structure inhibit students' progress at community colleges?* (CCRC Working Paper No. 25). New York, NY: Community College Research Center, Teachers College, Columbia University. Retrieved from http://ccrc.tc.columbia.edu/publications/lack-of-structure-students-progress.html

Swail, W. S., & Perna, L. W. (2002). Pre-college outreach programs. In W. G. Tierney & L. S. Hagedorn (Eds.), *Increasing access to college: Extending possibilities for all students* (pp. 15-34). Albany, NY: State University of New York Press.

Tinto, V. (2012). *Completing college: Rethinking institutional action*. Chicago, IL: University of Chicago Press.

UCF, IKM. (2016). *Student Success Project: Student performance analysis in course sequences at UCF*. Orlando, FL: University of Central Florida, Institutional Knowledge Management, IR32619, updated September 29, 2016.

Vance, J. D. (2016). *Hillbilly elegy: A memoir of a family and culture in crisis*. New York, NY: Harper Collins.

Wyner, J., Deane, K. C., Jenkins, D., & Fink, J. (2016). *The transfer playbook: Essential practices for two- and four-year colleges*. Retrieved from https://ccrc.tc.columbia.edu/media/k2/attachments/transfer-playbook-essential-practices.pdf

CHAPTER **4**
THEORIES, RESEARCH, AND **BEST PRACTICES RELATED** TO **TRANSFER STUDENT ORIENTATION**

Stephanie M. Foote

Although transfer students have experienced the initial transition to college, the move to a new institution can be challenging and, in some instances, result in "transfer shock" (decline in GPA), particularly for students transferring from two- to four-year institutions (Townsend & Wilson, 2006). The need to develop specialized orientation and transition experiences for transfer students has been well documented (Foote, Kranzow, & Hinkle, 2015; Hoover, 2010; Jacobs, 2004; Marling & Jacobs, 2011); however, the nuances that exist within the transfer student profile and pathways present challenges to these programs' development. Transfer students are diverse with respect to the number of credit hours transferred, age, number and type of institutions attended, academic preparation, personal commitments, and social identities (Hoover, 2010). Given the increasing numbers of students who have transferred at least once, estimated to be more than one third of the national undergraduate student population (Shapiro, Dundar, Wakhungu, Yuan, & Harrell, 2015), the need to reach transfer students has become increasingly important. Further, more than 80% of students enrolled at two-year institutions have indicated their intent to transfer to a four-year institution (Jenkins & Fink, 2016), suggesting the need to create dedicated transfer student orientation programs will remain high.

This chapter provides an introduction to theories, research, and best practices that can be used to guide the development and implementation of transfer student orientation programs. The chapter begins with a discussion of factors to consider in the development of such programs, followed by an overview of select student development theories with particular relevance to transfer students and examples to guide orientation practitioners as they apply these theories to practice. Examples of existing transfer student orientation programs, ranging from one-day sessions to transfer student seminars, are provided. The chapter ends with discussion of assessment of such programs.

Factors to Consider in the Development of Transfer Student Orientation Programs

A multitude of factors should be considered in developing transfer student orientation programs. This section describes some of those factors, including transfer student populations and identities, transfer paths and types of transfer, common transfer barriers, format options, and potential collaborations.

Transfer Student Populations and Transfer Student Identities

Understanding who transfer students are is foundational to developing orientation programs to meet their needs, both in content and format. Marling and Jacobs (2011) described the importance of developing an institutional profile that disaggregates transfer student data and provides "an accurate portrait" (p. 74) of an institution's transfer student population. They cited their experience with this task at the University of North Texas, which resulted in a "profile that contradicted faculty and staff perceptions of this population" (Marling & Jacobs, 2011, p. 74). An exercise of this type is vital in the development of transfer student orientation programs, and although these programs likely cannot be tailored to every transfer student population, they can be designed to be flexible and inclusive of multiple populations, sub-populations, and identity groups that might exist within an institution's transfer student population. For example, orientation programs for transfer students can be provided in different formats and lengths, as described in the "Models and Institutional Examples" section of this chapter, including opportunities for students to choose sessions that are most useful to them at the time.

Historically, colleges and universities have "categorize[d] transfer based on credit and degree attainment at the point of entry" (Aiken-Wisniewski, 2012, p. 50). However, simply identifying transfer students in this way does not account for the myriad personal attributes (e.g., gender, ethnicity, age), or background characteristics (e.g., employment, socioeconomic status, veteran, first-generation), that influence transfer student identity. Often assumptions are made about the needs of transfer students based on limited knowledge of the demographic composition of this population. For example, as Marling and Jacobs (2011) discovered, faculty and staff at their university assumed the majority of the transfer population were nontraditional, and they were surprised to learn that most of the transfers at that time were predominately undeclared sophomores, between the ages 19 and 24, who wanted to be involved in on-campus activities.

In the development of transfer student orientation programs, it is also essential to consider how aspects of the institutional environment and culture, including the language used to communicate with transfer students and institutional policies, practices, and traditions influence identity development and sense of belonging.

Moreover, it is important to examine the opportunities in these programs to create inclusive communities that allow students to reflect the intersections of their identities. In these programs, personal reflection might occur in the context of academic advising or in meetings with faculty members in the student's chosen major. Interactions with orientation leaders who are also transfer students can help foster a sense of belonging, which can be particularly important given the cultural and academic transitions transfer students often experience (Laanan, 2007; Townsend & Wilson, 2006). In addition to providing opportunities for personal reflection and interactions with peers, intentionally introducing transfer students to and engaging them in high-impact practices (HIPs) in the context of traditional or extended orientation experiences can positively impact student learning and engagement (Finley & McNair, 2013). Orientation programs provide a critical opportunity to introduce transfer students to HIPs, such as community engagement, study abroad, and undergraduate research. In addition to informing them of these opportunities, it is essential to engage transfer students in academic and cocurricular planning to determine how and where their participation in HIPs will occur in their undergraduate experience. This is particularly important because transfer students often participate in HIPs at lower rates than their peers (Finley & McNair, 2013; National Survey of Student Engagement, 2017).

It is also important to consider how communication with transfer students, both before and during orientation, relays aspects of the institutional culture and fosters belonging. In his research on the transfer student transition, Handel (2011) described transfer students as resembling "Alice in Wonderland [at a four-year campus]. They go from one place to another and have no clue about the culture of the institution" (p. 23). Herrera and Jain (2013) explain that it is essential for institutions to offer pre- and post-transfer initiatives that communicate a sense of welcome and transfer-receptive culture. Developing specific online and printed materials that communicate institutional culture in ways that are inclusive of transfer students begins to develop the cultural capital transfer students need to successfully navigate their new environment (Handel, 2011). A thorough examination of the language used in communications with incoming transfer students can provide insight into the ways that aspects of the institutional environment and culture are conveyed.

Transfer Paths and Types of Transfer

Transfer pathways have become increasingly complex and diverse given the "blurring ways in which transfer occurs" (Wang, 2017, p. 7). Aiken-Wisniewski (2012) identified several categories of transfer: (a) vertical or transfer up (transfer from a two- to a four-year institution), (b) lateral (transfer between two-year institutions or four-year institutions), (c) reverse (transfer from a four- to a two-year institution), (d) swirler (movement between multiple institutions), and (e) thwarted transfers (students who are unable to enter institutions or experience problems transferring credits because of the absence of articulation agreements (p. 50). In addition to the types of transfer, McCormick (2003) identified eight emerging enrollment patterns that provide a more nuanced insight into swirling (i.e., concurrent enrollment at multiple institutions): trial enrollment, special program enrollment, supplemental enrollment, rebounding enrollment, concurrent enrollment (also known as double dipping), consolidated enrollment, serial transfer, and independent enrollment.

In examining transfer paths and types of transfer, it is also important to consider both internal and external transfers. *External transfers* are those students coming from a different institution that might be referred to as the sending institution to a new receiving institution. *Internal transfers* may be students transferring to another academic major, department, or college within an institution (Aiken-Wisniewski, 2012) or within a university system to another campus. Although the existing research and literature tends to focus on external transfers, depending on the organizational structure of the institution, it is possible that internal transfer students can experience academic, social, or cultural transitions similar to those of external transfers (Aiken-Wisniewski, 2012). In the context of developing orientation programs for transfer students or enhancing existing programs, understanding the type(s) of transfer path or experience might also provide valuable insight into transfer student identity and motivation.

Common Barriers

Although transfer students have experience with the process of higher education and may understand how their sending institution works, they have varying levels of *transfer student capital*, or the "accumulation of knowledge and skills that are essential and unique to the transfer process" (Handel, 2011, p. 415). Access to transfer capital may also influence their transition. Specifically, transfer student capital is influenced by the extent that students are prepared for and familiar with academic requirements at the receiving institution, as well as the extent to which they understand articulation agreements (documents that describe how and which credits will transfer and where these credits will count) between their sending and receiving institutions. Populations of transfer students, particularly those transferring from two- to four-year institutions, may lack the highly specialized knowledge they need to negotiate the "distinct and sometimes oppositional academic cultures" (Handel, 2011, p. 415) that exist at these two types of institutions. Thus, the capital for students transferring from two- to four-year institutions may be less than that of their transfer peers.

Often, transfer students look to the sending and receiving institutions to help them navigate the transition. However, even when articulation agreements exist between institutions, other policies and practices may present additional and often unintended barriers in the transfer transition, including limited access to classes and campus services for students enrolled in evening, weekend, or online classes. In addition, institutional policies that impact credit hour transfer or enrollment might contribute to lost credits or "leakage" that has become common among students moving from two- to four-year institutions (Bradley, 2014). Institutional obstacles are just one influence on student participation in learning activities. Cross (1981) also noted situational (conditions at a specific time) and dispositional (student perceptions about personal abilities) barriers as significantly impacting student learning. Bean and Metzner's (1985) taxonomy of barriers to persistence help explain how external forces, including academic and environmental variables, influence the success of nontraditional or transfer students.

While transfer student orientation programs cannot mitigate all of the potential barriers to learning, these experiences can be designed, both in content and format, to respond to the unique transitions these students experience, and they can help remove some of the aforementioned common barriers. Specifically, some of the common obstacles can be overcome by providing students information about and access to institutional resources, including academic advisors and faculty in the student's major. Connecting new transfer students to these resources early, even before they officially transfer, can be essential to their transition. Kennesaw State University's Transfer Advocate Gateway (TAG, n.d.) program embeds enrollment service specialists at two-year feeder institutions to provide consistent support to students prior to their transfer transition. Transfer centers (physical and virtual) and transfer guides can help provide similar types of support.

Format Options

Given the diversity within the transfer student population, it is essential to provide orientation programs customized to meet the unique needs of the students they serve, but it is also vital to offer these programs in different formats. Marling and Jacobs (2011) explain that orientation programs reaffirm a transfer student's decision to attend the institution, but to be most effective these programs must be developed with consideration of these students' diverse needs. Replicating an existing first-year orientation program and offering it to transfer students does not adequately attend to their needs, nor does it help ameliorate the tendency of students to think of it as just another orientation experience (Marling & Jacobs, 2011).

In the 2017 NODA Databank survey of orientation, transition, and retention professionals, 87% of respondents indicated they had specialized orientation programs for transfer students, and about half indicated their programs were mandatory, with the majority occurring during the summer and winter. Those programs tended to be of limited duration, with 79% of respondents reporting programs that were one full day or less. However, just over 21% of respondents reported programs that were between 1½ and three or more days in length (NODA, 2017). Specific content in the reported programs differed based on program length, timing, and goals, but many included some form of academic advising and an introduction to campus resources and services, often culminating with student course registration. Longer or multi-day transfer student orientation programs tended to include more opportunities for interactions with peers, faculty, and staff at the institution, as well as dedicated time for history, traditions, and social activities.

In addition to differences in the length of time and specific content of these programs, the mode of delivery varied. For example, some programs were delivered fully or partially online, at a satellite location (sometimes the sending institution), and on evenings and weekends. In developing these programs, it is important to consider opportunities to use a variety of modalities to offer all or part of the orientation experience. For example, online orientation modules can provide information to transfer students who might not to be able to attend a full- or multi-day program. Moreover, offering orientation programs at satellite locations might be useful to students, particularly those at two-year institutions, who are preparing to transfer.

Collaborations

While collaboration is common to all orientation programs, creating a truly transfer-receptive culture requires involving a variety of functional areas and departments in the development and implementation of programs focusing on transfer student orientation. Marling and Jacobs (2011) encourage establishing a cross-functional orientation planning committee with transfer student representation; they stress the importance of committee members who are knowledgeable about and sensitive to the needs of transfer students. Because the transfer student experience begins pre-transfer, it is important to foster relationships with sending institutions, particularly two-year colleges that might be considered feeder institutions, to ensure that students who intend to transfer have the information they need. To facilitate communication and collaboration between the sending and receiving institutions, orientation professionals might consider inviting representatives from two-year institutions to participate in periodic meetings of the cross-functional orientation planning committee. Additionally, collaboration across functional areas allows orientation professionals to advocate for ample course availability at transfer student orientation, timely processing of transfer credit evaluation, and academic advisor training to ensure all faculty and staff advisors are familiar with academic programs and procedures.

Using Student Development Theories to Guide Development of Transfer Orientation Programs

Student development theories can be foundational to the development of all orientation programs and particularly for those aimed at transfer students. As Patton, Renn, Guido, Quaye, and Evans (2016) describe, student development theories help practitioners and scholars understand how students "grow and develop holistically, with increased complexity" (p. 6), and they largely describe positive growth and change that occur during the higher education experience (Jones & Abes, 2011). While many theories may be useful to orientation practitioners, this section provides a brief overview of several student development theories that are particularly relevant to the development of transfer student orientation programs.

Chickering's Theory of Identity Development

With an explicit focus on identity formation, Chickering's theory (Chickering & Reisser, 1993) examines the psychosocial development of college students and the influence of aspects of the environment on that developmental process (Patton et al., 2016). Development occurs as students move "through cycles of challenge and response, differentiation and integration, and disequilibrium and regained equilibrium" (Chickering & Reisser, 1993, p. 476). This movement is punctuated by a progression through the following seven vectors that account for aspects of emotional, interpersonal, intellectual, and ethical development (Patton et al., 2016):

1. Developing competence,
2. Managing emotions,
3. Moving through autonomy toward interdependence,
4. Developing mature interpersonal relationships,
5. Establishing identity,
6. Developing purpose, and
7. Developing integrity.

Chickering and Reisser's (1993) theory lends itself to the development of orientation programs because as Rode and Cawthon (2010) indicate, early college students, particularly first- and second-year students, are actively experiencing the vectors, although it is important to note that the rate they do so will vary based on the individual student. Moreover, the aspects of development addressed in each vector align with many of the common academic and social transition components of transfer orientation programs described in the 2017 NODA Databank survey. Given the diversity within most transfer student populations, it is impossible to place these students in any specific vector; however, for students who are transferring after their second year, it is more likely that they are focused on interpersonal relationships, identity, purpose, and integrity. With this in mind, it is important to consider the extent that orientation programs provide transfer students with opportunities: to develop relationships with their peers and with faculty and staff, and to explore and acknowledge aspects of their identity, belonging, and motivation.

Transition Theory

Although adults constantly experience transitions, how they respond depends on situation factors (Goodman, Schlossberg, & Anderson, 2006) that often include timing, duration, previous experience with similar transitions, and concurrent stress. Despite the unique situational factors, Schlossberg's transition theory is useful in orientation planning and implementation because it provides insight into how adults navigate the transition process; it also gives context to help understand the ways a person responds to a specific transition (e.g., enrolling in a new institution) the first, second, or third time it is experienced. The transfer transition will happen more than once for some students and as situational factors vary, so will their responses. Personal perceptions of significance influence how an individual experiences a transition, and "when an individual perceives a transition to be significant, it may result in changes in behaviors and relationships" (Foote et al., 2013, p. 6).

Transition can be defined as an event or non-event that can result in changes in behaviors and relationships. The transition model (Goodman et al., 2006) examines the external and personal factors that influence transition, as well as institutional responses for strategies to help individuals through various transitions. The model is composed of the following three parts:

- *Approaching transitions* identifies the type of transition (anticipated, unanticipated, and non-event transitions), the context of the transition, and the potential impact on the person experiencing the transition.

- *Taking stock of coping resources* includes what Goodman et al. (2006) refer to as the 4 S System (situation, self, social support, and strategies or coping resources), which includes factors that affect a person's ability to handle the change that comes with the transition process.

- *Taking charge* refers to the individual in transition using new strategies to achieve a level of control of the situation.

The components or moments in the transition model can be used to structure orientation programs that provide support as students prepare to transfer through early advising and transcript review; through intentional introduction to support services, faculty, and staff; and through opportunities to develop relationships with peers during and post-transfer.

Perry's Theory of Intellectual and Ethical Development

Perry's (1968) theory of intellectual and ethical development provides a schematic from which to understand how an individual sees the world and how that perspective is influenced by three modes of meaning making: dualism (i.e., an individual views the world as good or bad, right or wrong), multiplicity (i.e., an individual recognizes diverse viewpoints), and relativism (i.e., an individual views knowledge contextually and understands not all opinions or ideas are valid). The progression in meaning making is signified by experiences that foster cognitive dissonance, and in turn, prompt movement through the nine positions in Perry's theory (Patton et al., 2016).

Understanding Perry's theory can help professional and student orientation staff be prepared to work with any student or family member, but in particular, transfer student orientation experiences can be designed with the goal of fostering students' cognitive development and using Perry's theory as a guide. Engaging in problem-solving activities or attending mini lectures (in a student's chosen academic major) during orientation, or taking part in integrated activities and assignments related to content in a virtual orientation, can all potentially contribute to a student's intellectual and ethical development.

Social Identities

As Patton et al. (2016) describe, social identities provide "a central organizing concept for understanding self in society, and in the context of higher education, as a foundation for understanding student development" (p. 71). Social identities can include gender, race, sexual orientation, and ability, and as Rode and Cawthon (2010) indicate, social identities reveal "the complexity of identity during the college years" (p. 16), which extends beyond psychosocial and cognitive structural development. The theories and models associated with social identity development can be traced back to social movements (e.g., the civil rights movement, the feminist movement), and foundational to these concepts of social identity is "how individuals make meaning of the world they occupy" (Patton et al., 2016, p. 75). In the context of transfer student orientation programs, it is important to provide all students with information about the services, programs, and student organizations connected to social identity groups. Further, it is important to examine printed materials, presentations, and scripts from transfer orientation programs to ensure the language, images, and speakers are sensitive to and inclusive of a wide range of social identity groups.

Intersectionality

In addition to understanding social identity development, it is useful for faculty and staff members who work with orientation programs for transfer students to consider the concept of *intersectionality*, a construct from which to examine how identities intersect and contribute to aspects of individual development (Patton et al., 2016). In discussing types of transfer student populations and identities, intersectionality can help shed light on "the importance of connections and relationships, rather than attending primarily to isolated and individual factors, like race and gender" (Barnett & Felten, 2016, p. 137). As Dooley and LePeau (2016) describe, "Students' experiences at colleges and universities are often interpreted and understood through the lens of a single aspect of their identity (e.g., race, gender, disability, or social class) without regard to other aspects of identity, nor to the salience that dimension of identity has to the student" (p. 66). With transfer students, one identity may be more prevalent than another, and identity salience can be influenced by environmental factors.

Models and Institutional Examples of Transfer Orientation Programs

As the previous sections in this chapter demonstrate, there are many considerations to be made in the development and implementation of a transfer student orientation program. These programs should be customized, in content and delivery, well timed given the transfer transition experience, and inclusive of the myriad identities transfer students claim. Many different approaches to transfer student orientation exist, as the 2017 NODA Databank survey responses suggest, and this section will describe several different institutional approaches to the transfer orientation process.

University at Albany (Multi-Day Transfer Orientation)

The University at Albany, part of the State University of New York (SUNY), is a public research university that enrolls approximately 17,000 undergraduate and graduate students. About one third of the university's incoming class and half of its graduating class is composed of transfer students from a variety of institutional and demographic backgrounds (e.g., transfers from two-year and four-year institutions, students seeking second degrees, and traditional and nontraditional in age) (Flynn-Barker, Malatesta, Khatib, & Nyman, 2016). The university transitioned from a one-day orientation program that focused on advisement and course registration to a two-day program that provided students opportunities to learn about campus involvement, be welcomed into the university community, and bond with their transfer peers (Flynn-Barker et al., 2016). Orientation staff conducted research on transfer orientation programs at peer institutions, met with campus stakeholders, and used feedback from current transfer students to re-envision the approach to transfer orientation at the university. The question, *What do transfer students need and when?* was foundational in developing the new transfer orientation program (Flynn-Barker et al., 2016).

The program is composed of two parts: Transfer Advisement and Transfer Orientation. Advisement takes place throughout the summer and students choose one of five dates to attend; it includes meetings with academic advisors, information sessions, and optional campus tours. During the second part of the orientation process, which occurs the Friday before classes begin, students choose from several "conference style" presentations on a variety of topics, including talking with faculty, getting involved in undergraduate research, things to do and see in the city, Greek life, and sexual health (Flynn-Barker et al., 2016). Students have reported satisfaction with Transfer Advisement and Orientation, and as a result of the revisions to the program, they have also indicated an increased knowledge of campus resources (Flynn-Barker et al., 2016).

University of Iowa (Orientation and Success at Iowa Course)

The University of Iowa is a large research university with an undergraduate enrollment of approximately 23,300 and a transfer enrollment of 1,056. All new, incoming students (first-year and transfer) must attend an in-person orientation (Arthur & Wiebel, 2016). In-person, day-long transfer orientation sessions consist mostly of academic advising and course registration, but in 2014 the institution created an advisory board to help develop an online experience to supplement the in-person orientation for new transfer students (Arthur & Wiebel, 2016). As a result, the two-credit hour, required (for all new students), online CS 1600: Success at Iowa course was developed. The course consists of four parts, with the first occurring before orientation, the second coming post-orientation, the third occurring on the first day of the semester, and the fourth occurring three to four weeks into the semester. The four parts consist of multiple modules that span a range of topics, including an introduction to the university (pre-orientation), an overview of the learning management system and other technology (pre- and post-orientation), information about plagiarism (post-orientation and first day of the semester), and other strategies for success at the university (Arthur & Wiebel, 2016).

In 2016, a transfer-specific section of the CS 1600 course was implemented, and along with developing the transfer section, the university created a Transfer Support Team and instituted a transition survey, Excelling@Iowa, with transfer-specific messaging (Arthur & Caskey, 2016). Institutional data from the course have helped the university identify students potentially at risk of not persisting, and the course and survey have revealed some common transitional issues that all new students, including transfers, experience. Those issues have been used to create new modules (e.g., Housing and Navigating Campus) and messaging to further differentiate the course from the in-person orientation (Arthur & Wiebel, 2016).

Stockton University (Transfer Student Seminar)

Stockton University, located in New Jersey, enrolls approximately 8,674 students, with 1,052 transfer and readmitted students (Stockton University, n.d.). The university has offered a variety of first-year seminars across the general studies curriculum, and in 2003 Stockton adapted that approach to create transfer student seminars (Foote & Grites, 2017). Rather than offering a new, general transfer student seminar, faculty who were teaching courses in the general studies curriculum were invited to teach a dedicated section of their course for transfer students. Faculty who teach the designated transfer sections of their courses incorporate content and assignments to help students become connected to the university and to their peers, faculty, and staff. Since 2003, courses across the disciplines have been taught as transfer seminars, including: Contemporary American Education, Marketing Principles, Cognitive Psychology, Research Designs and Methods in Criminal Justice, and History's Mysteries (Foote & Grites, 2017).

Although transfer students are not required to take a course designated as a transfer seminar, given the number and range of offerings in the general studies curriculum, the majority do take a seminar in their first semester at the university. Of those who take a designated transfer seminar course, retention and progression rates are higher compared with transfer students who do not take such a course (Foote & Grites, 2017).

Assessment of Transfer Orientation Programs

The assessment and evaluation of orientation programs has become commonplace, and as Schwartz and Wiese (2010) indicate, an orientation assessment and evaluation plan "can help to demonstrate their vital contributions to student and institutional success for both internal and external audiences" (p. 217). Upcraft and Schuh (1996) describe assessment as "any effort to gather, analyze, and interpret evidence which describes institutional or departmental effectiveness" (p. 18), and evaluation is defined as "any effort to use assessment evidence to improve institutional or departmental effectiveness" (Upcraft & Schuh, 1996, p. 19). Assessment and program evaluation data can help inform improvements to existing orientation programs and guide the development of new initiatives. This section will describe some of the approaches for assessing transfer orientation programs, including the use of the Council for the Advancement of Standards in Higher Education's (CAS) standards for orientation programs and transfer student programs and services, measurement of student learning outcomes, and program evaluation.

CAS Standards, Assessment, and Program Evaluation

Founded in 1979, CAS promotes "standards in student affairs, student services, and student development programs. CAS creates and delivers dynamic, credible standards, guidelines, and Self-Assessment Guides that are designed to lead a host of quality programs and services" (CAS, n.d.). The CAS standards represent 45 functional areas, including orientation programs and transfer student programs and services. While the standards vary by functional area, there are consistent categories of student learning and development domains (e.g., knowledge acquisition, integration, construction, and application; cognitive complexity; intrapersonal development; interpersonal competence; humanitarianism and civic engagement; and practical competence) and dimensions across program and service areas (CAS, 2009). To apply the standards, functional areas identify learning outcomes that map to the domains, collect outcome data, and then identify and describe how the specific services or programs in that area contribute to the student learning outcomes. CAS also offers self-assessment guides (SAGs) to facilitate program review and evaluation.

The CAS standards for orientation programs and transfer student programs and services articulate a shared commitment to the transition of students to their new institutional environment. Moreover, both sets of standards speak to the goal of creating intentional experiences that are designed specifically for the populations they serve, including varying the modalities and contexts in which the programs are offered, with the intention of fostering student learning and development in both the curriculum and cocurriculum. Both sets of standards also describe the programs and services as providing continuous experiences that deliver pathways for the students they serve, which ultimately contribute to student transition and success. In the context of transfer orientation programs, the CAS standards can first be used to develop program goals and outcomes and then to identify the measures that will be used to evaluate outcomes.

Once learning outcomes have been identified, an important step in the assessment process is to map the outcomes to components of the transfer orientation program (Lingren Clark & Cinoman, 2014). The mapping process is useful because it both aligns the student learning outcomes to specific aspects of the program, but it also potentially illuminates areas where alignment is lacking. Lingren Clark and Cinoman (2014) suggest that orientation professionals conduct a gap analysis to identify holes in the program content and to determine how these might be addressed in other programming. It is also important to identify how the outcomes will be measured and the places in the transfer orientation process where those data are collected.

Assessment data can be used to engage in program evaluation, which involves using the data to improve the overall effectiveness of a transfer orientation program. As Marling and Jacobs (2011) indicate, it is important to use assessment data to critically examine transfer student orientation programs and determine whether minor or significant adjustments need to be made to existing programs. Often, student satisfaction data provide valuable insight into aspects of the orientation program that may need improvement, and it is important to share these data and related recommendations with the other faculty and staff involved in the design and delivery of transfer student orientation programs.

The office of Orientation & First-Year Programs (OFYP) at the University of Minnesota has created a first-year assessment plan that begins with a pre-orientation student survey and includes the collection of a variety of formal or primary and secondary data to evaluate outcomes associated with participation in their programs, as well as the overall new student experience, student satisfaction, and aspects of retention and matriculation (Orientation & First-Year Programs, n.d.). Although the assessment plan is aimed at the first-year student experience, the OFYP staff have adapted aspects of this assessment process to evaluate outcomes of their transfer programs and the transfer student experience at the university. Essential to the assessment process, the OFYP staff continuously use the data collected through their assessment cycle to examine outcomes of specific programs in the department and to develop a more robust understanding of the new student experience at the university.

Conclusion

The development and implementation of specialized transfer student orientation programs is essential to the transition of this growing student population. Although transfer students have experienced the initial transition to college, moving to a new college or university can be challenging, particularly for students transferring from two- to four-year institutions. Without the benefit of a dedicated transfer student orientation experience, students may lack the transfer capital vital to their success. Removing institutional barriers and communicating policies and procedures, including the transferability of credits from the sending to the receiving institution, is another important aspect of the transfer student orientation process and demonstrates a transfer-receptive culture. Both sending and receiving institutions play an important role in the transition and success of transfer students, and to that end, each institution must ensure that they communicate with transfer students.

As Marling and Jacobs (2011) indicate, transfer student success is an institution-wide effort; as such, faculty, staff, and students need to be involved and engaged in that process. Transfer student orientation programs should be designed to be inclusive of the different functional areas and individuals essential to transfer student transition. Attention should also be given to the ways that transfer students are welcomed into the institutional culture, including examining communication with incoming transfers, both before and during orientation, to determine how these communications relay aspects of the institutional culture and foster sense of belonging. Moreover, it is important to examine the opportunities in these programs to create inclusive communities that allow students to reflect the intersections of their identities. By developing transfer student orientation programs that consider student demographics and identities, along with pathways to and through the transfer transition, while also providing customized content in a variety of delivery modes, institutions can truly begin to meet the nuanced needs of their transfer student population.

References

Aiken-Wisniewski, S. A. (2012). Types of transfer students. In T. Grites & C. Duncan (Eds.). *Advising transfer students: Strategies for today's realities and tomorrow's challenges* (2nd ed., pp. 37-57). Manhattan, KS: NACADA.

Arthur, T., & Caskey, B. (2016). *The crossroads: Creating successful transfer student transitions.* Presentation at the 2016 NODA Annual Conference. Louisville, KY.

Arthur, T., & Wiebel, C. (2016). *OTR: Crossroads of an online transition course and early intervention strategies.* Presentation at the 2016 NODA Annual Conference. Louisville, KY.

Barnett, B., & Felten, P. (2016). *Intersectionality in action: A guide for faculty and campus leaders for creating inclusive classrooms and institutions.* Sterling, VA: Stylus.

Bean, J., & Metzner, B. (1985). A conceptual model of nontraditional student attrition. *Review of Educational Research, 55,* 485-540.

Bradley, P. (2014, May 6). Plugging the pipeline: Colleges seek to improve transfer policies and practices. *Community College Week,* 6-8.

Chickering, A. W., & Reisser, L. (1993). *Education and identity* (2nd ed.). San Francisco, CA: Jossey-Bass.

Council for the Advancement of Standards in Higher Education (CAS). (n.d.). *Standards.* Retrieved from http://www.cas.edu/standards

Council for the Advancement of Standards in Higher Education (CAS). (2009). CAS learning and development outcomes. In L. A. Dean (Ed.), *CAS professional standards for higher education* (7th ed.). Washington, DC: Author.

Cross, K. P. (1981). *Adults as learners: Increasing participation and facilitating learning.* San Francisco, CA: Jossey-Bass.

Dooley, J., & LePeau, L. (2016). Striving for an inclusive and nurturing campus: Cultivating the intersections. In B. Barnett & P. Felten (Eds.), *Intersectionality in action: A guide for faculty and campus leaders for creating inclusive classrooms and institutions* (pp. 63-76). Sterling, VA: Stylus.

Finley, A., & McNair, T. (2013). *Assessing underserved students' engagement in high-impact practices.* Washington, DC: Association of American Colleges & Universities.

Flynn-Barker, H., Malatesta, J., Khatib, S., & Nyman, M. (2016). *One size doesn't fit all: Transforming transfer orientation.* Presentation at the 2016 NODA Annual Conference. Louisville, KY.

Foote, S. M., & Grites, T. J. (2017). *Maximizing transfer student transitions and success in the classroom.* Presentation at the 15th Annual Conference of the National Institute for the Study of Transfer Students. Atlanta, GA.

Foote, S. M., Hinkle, S., Kranzow, J., Pistilli, M., Rease Miles, L., & Simmons, J. (2013). *College students in transition: An annotated bibliography.* Columbia, SC: University of South Carolina, National Resource Center for The First-Year Experience and Students in Transition.

Foote, S. M., Kranzow, J., & Hinkle, S. (2015). Focusing on the forgotten: An examination of the influences and innovative practices that affect community college transfer student success. In S. J. Jones & D. L. Jackson (Eds.), *Examining the impact of community colleges on the global workforce* (pp. 94-124). Hershey, PA: Information Science Reference (IGI Global).

Goodman, J., Schlossberg, N. K., & Anderson, M. L. (2006). *Counseling adult students in transition: Linking theory with practice* (3rd ed.). New York, NY: Springer.

Handel, S. J. (2011). *Improving student transfer from community colleges to four-year institutions: The perspective of leaders from baccalaureate-granting institutions.* New York, NY: College Board.

Herrera, A., & Jain, D. (2013). Building a transfer-receptive culture at four-year institutions. *New Directions for Higher Education, 162,* 51-59.

Hoover, S. C. (2010). Designing orientation and transition programs for transfer students. In J. Ward-Roof (Ed.), *Designing successful transitions: A guide for orienting students to college* (Monograph No. 13, 3rd ed., pp. 181-192). Columbia, SC: University of South Carolina, National Resource Center for The First-Year Experience and Students in Transition.

Jacobs, B. C. (2004). Today's transfer students: Trends and challenges. In B. C. Jacobs (Ed.), *The college transfer student in America: The forgotten student* (pp. 1-14). Washington, DC: The American Association of Collegiate Registrars and Admissions Officers (AACRAO).

Jenkins, D., & Fink, J. (2016, January). *Tracking transfer: New measures of institutional and state effectiveness in helping community college students attain bachelor's degrees.* New York, NY: Community College Resource Center, Teachers College, Columbia University. Retrieved from http://ccrc.tc.columbia.edu/publications/tracking-transfer-institutional-state-effectiveness.html

Jones, S. R., & Abes, E. S. (2011). The nature and use of theory. In J. H. Schuh, S. R. Jones, & S. Harper (Eds.), *Student services: A handbook for the profession* (5th ed., pp. 149-167). San Francisco, CA: Jossey-Bass.

Laanan, F. S. (2007). Studying transfer students: Part II: Dimensions of transfer students' adjustment. *Community College Journal of Research and Practice, 31*(1), 37-59.

Lingren Clark, B. M., & Cinoman, A. H. (2014). Assessing and evaluating orientation and retention programs. In the *Orientation Planning Manual* (pp. 113-122). Minneapolis, MN: The Association for Orientation, Transition, and Retention in Higher Education (NODA).

Marling, J. L., & Jacobs, B. C. (2011). Establishing pathways for transfer student success through orientation. In M. A. Poisel & S. Joseph (Eds.), *Transfer students in higher education: Building foundations for policies, programs, and services that foster student success* (Monograph No. 54, pp. 71-87). Columbia, SC: University of South Carolina, National Resource Center for The First-Year Experience and Students in Transition.

McCormick, A. C. (2003). Swirling and double-dipping: New patterns of student attendance and their implications for higher education. In J. E. King, E. L. Anderson, & M. E. Corrigan (Eds.), *Changing student attendance patterns: Challenges for policy and practice* (New Directions for Higher Education No. 121, pp. 13-24). San Francisco, CA: Jossey-Bass.

National Survey of Student Engagement (2017). *Engagement insights: Survey findings on the quality of undergraduate education – annual results 2017.* Bloomington, IN: Indiana University Center for Postsecondary Research. Retrieved from http://nsse.indiana.edu/NSSE_2017_Results/pdf/NSSE_2017_Annual_Results.pdf

NODA–Association for Admissions, Orientation, and Transition in Higher Education (2017). *Databank.* Retrieved from http://www.nodaweb.org/page/Databank

Orientation & First-Year Programs at the University of Minnesota (n.d.). *First-year assessment.* Retrieved from https://www.ofyp.umn.edu/more/first-year-assessment

Patton, L. D., Renn, K. A., Guido, F. M., Quaye, S. J., & Evans, N. J., (2016). *Student development in college: Theory, research, and practice* (3rd ed.). San Francisco, CA: Jossey-Bass.

Perry, W. G. (1968). *Forms of intellectual and ethical development in the college years: A scheme.* New York, NY: Holt, Rinehart, & Winston.

Rode, D. L., & Cawthon, T. W. (2010). Theoretical perspectives on orientation. In J. Ward-Roof (Ed.), *Designing successful transitions: A guide for orienting students to college* (Monograph No. 13, 3rd ed., pp. 11-28). Columbia, SC: University of South Carolina, National Resource Center for The First-Year Experience and Students in Transition.

Schwartz, R., & Wiese, D. (2010). Assessment and evaluation in orientation. In J. Ward-Roof (Ed.), *Designing successful transitions: A guide for orienting students to college* (Monograph No. 13, 3rd ed., pp. 217-228). Columbia, SC: University of South Carolina, National Resource Center for The First-Year Experience and Students in Transition.

Shapiro, D., Dundar, A., Wakhungu, P.K, Yuan, X., & Harrell, A. (2015, July). *Transfer and mobility: A national view of student movement in postsecondary institutions, fall 2008 cohort* (Signature Report No. 9). Herndon, VA: National Student Clearinghouse Research Center.

Stockton University (n.d.). *About Stockton.* Retrieved from https://www.stockton.edu/about-stockton/index.html

Townsend, B. K., & Wilson, K. B. (2006). A hand hold for a little bit: Factors facilitating the success of community college transfer students to a large research university. *Journal of College Student Development, 47*(4), 439–456.

Transfer Advocate Gateway Program at Kennesaw State University (n.d.). *TAG program overview.* Retrieved from http://grants.kennesaw.edu/tag/about/program-overview.php

Upcraft, M. L., & Schuh, J. H. (1996). *Assessment in student affairs: A guide for practitioners.* San Francisco, CA: Jossey-Bass.

Wang, X. (2017). Editor's note. *New Directions for Institutional Research, 170,* 7-8.

CHAPTER 5
ACADEMIC ADVISING FOR STUDENT MOBILITY |

Carol A. Van Der Karr

As discussed in earlier chapters, transfer students follow many paths and face the challenges of navigating multiple curricula, policies, and structures in order to be successful. Amid the strategies to support transfer students, effective advising is a powerful tool in helping each student manage their unique experience and maximize their opportunities (Drake, 2011).

The ability of students to move between institutions successfully and attain degrees has implications for the students themselves, colleges and systems, as well as potential to promote equity and address issues of social stratification (Lumina Foundation for Education, 2009). As more students attend multiple colleges, there is greater need for higher education institutions to make transferring a viable, cost-effective, and quality educational experience. Even with louder calls from students, government leaders, and educational institutions to improve transfer mobility and degree attainment, significant questions remain about the best practices to enhance educational opportunities for all students.

Efforts to increase mobility often focus on system and state policies related to program and course articulations and admissions. These efforts are designed to be broad-based and cost-effective solutions in order to support the greatest number of students. The impact of policy is limited because it is based on a model of the ideal transfer experience. That is, policy may benefit certain types of transfer students more because it does not fully take into account the career exploration and change of major, stop-out and readmission, and academic development that define the postsecondary education experience for many students. Similarly, technology can be a powerful means for mobility by providing access to information and coordinating data sharing among institutions, but students need support in accessing and fully using the tools to gain the benefit of the technologies.

Campus-based institutional practices and policies may have more direct impact on student experiences than statewide or system initiatives. Direct support to students through academic advising and other counseling supports are found to positively influence the transfer experience (Hood, Hunt, & Haeffele, 2009). Institutional services, such as advisement, can increase student success by connecting the students with academic information and assistance, supporting integration into the campus and guiding students as they navigate new processes and experiences (Flaga, 2006).

This chapter will discuss the ways advising can anticipate, plan for, and respond to the major challenges of transfers as a cohort and as individual students. The chapter will start with a review of transfer mobility issues relevant to advising including curriculum and credit evaluation, academic preparation, and navigation of a new institutional culture. This is followed by a discussion of the implications and strategies for advisors working with transfer students. Finally, it will address how advising intersects with other campus services and how advisors can be advocates and collaborators with colleagues, both on campus and at partner institutions.

Transfer Advising: Challenges and Context

Understanding the common trends and issues of transfer students is foundational in the design and delivery of effective transfer student advising. It is also critical in demonstrating how advising initiatives can mitigate challenges and support advocacy for transfer-specific programs. This starts with understanding the different types of transfer enrollment patterns. Initially, discussion of transfer was focused solely on students moving from a two-year to a four-year institution, but transfer is now seen in several directions (e.g., reverse, lateral) and often includes attendance at more than two institutions. Additionally, students may cycle between levels of institutions, swirling back and forth between two- and four-year colleges before completing a degree (McGuire & Belcheir, 2013). Demographically, compared with students who start at a four-year college, transfers are more likely to be first-generation, come from families with a lower socioeconomic status, and be from traditionally underrepresented cultural and ethnic groups (Chen, 2016). Understanding the demographics of transfer students and having adequate institutional supports to respond to their needs is key to transfer success (Marling, 2013).

Common challenges for transfer students include loss of credits when transferring, extended time to degree, lack of access to financial aid and housing, adjustment to new environment, and poor academic performance (Eggleston & Laanan, 2001; Pascarella & Terenzini, 2005). Challenges most relevant to academic advising can be conceptualized into the following three areas: (a) curriculum, credits, and planning; (b) academic preparedness and transfer shock; and (c) navigating a new institutional culture.

Curriculum, Credits, and Planning

Transfer involves understanding the complexity of program requirements across multiple institutions along with their propensity for change. External accreditations, professional regulations, and campus- or system-driven expansion of major and general education have complicated undergraduate degree requirements. As a result, students experience a more prescriptive set of requirements, fewer electives, and more rigid sequencing of courses. Complexities of curricula make aligning programs and majors across multiple institutions a daunting task. Yet, alignment of institutional administrative processes is linked to efficient transfer and degree completion (Hood et al., 2009, Simone, 2014).

To be successful, transfer students must know the requirements of their first academic program, those of the transfer institution, and the ways those curricula converge and diverge. Sources of information, such as college catalogs and advising planning sheets, vary by campus and program, making the entirety of information difficult to decipher, or even access, at times. Students increasingly attend more than two colleges before completing their undergraduate degree, compounding the curriculum challenge (Doyle, 2006; Hagedorn et al., 2006).

Credit evaluation processes have a significant impact on students' ability to transfer and their subsequent time to degree at the four-year institution. The review of transfer equivalencies can be organized into two phases: (a) identifying individual course equivalencies (e.g., Institution X's Introduction to Writing is equivalent to Institution Y's Composition Introduction) and (b) determining how those credits apply to the degree the transfer student is now seeking. For example, a student may have taken a public speaking course that has a direct equivalent at their new college. Yet, the presence of an equivalent course is no guarantee that it will satisfy requirements for a specific degree. Perhaps the degree requirements at the receiving institution are more prescriptive, and the public speaking course does not satisfy requirements for the desired degree. The degree audit may reveal that of the 60 hours accepted for transfer, only 45 can be applied to the degree sought. The result is that the student who anticipated spending four more semesters in college now realizes it will take an additional semester, year, or more to complete their degree. Clarifying the difference between *Does this course have an equivalency?* and *Does this course apply to my new degree?* is often the first task that advisors work through with new transfer students.

For students to navigate the credit evaluation process, they need access to accurate information, to understand the policy and processes, and be active self-advocates throughout. Some colleges maintain published course equivalency tables that help students see the relationship between courses at one school to another. The sheer number of courses and dynamic nature of curriculum require extensive oversight to keep these equivalencies current.

Campuses can assist students by assuring that credit evaluation processes are easily accessible, have clear parameters and rationale, include timelines, allow for discussion and reevaluation when reasonable, and have a contact person/office to assist students. Advisors working with students intending to transfer can help students find this information, assist with understanding the credit evaluation decisions, and mentor students on how to advocate for themselves.

Students' clarity on their career and major goals is particularly important as transfer students work within a more limited timeframe. The earlier students can identify their interests, assess their abilities, and connect those to career goals, the more effectively they can plan their coursework. Early advising initiatives focusing on career exploration and decision making lead to more effective academic planning across institutions. The challenge for advisors is to encourage students to work toward clarity on career goals while allowing them the time to make well-informed decisions and explore coursework that helps clarify goals.

Academic Preparedness and Transfer Shock

Academic preparedness has been examined from several perspectives, with the consensus that previous educational experiences and incoming competencies do affect transfer student success. High school academic background relates to faster time to transfer (Roksa & Calcagno, 2008), and higher semester GPA at time of transfer correlates to greater persistence and degree attainment at the transfer institution (Bowen, Chingos, & McPherson, 2009; Ishitani, 2008; Wang, 2012).

The academic transition for transfers is affected by gaps in academic skills, access to resources, shift to upper-division coursework, and adjustment to new academic culture and expectations. Gaps in preparedness are often identified at the first institution but may not be closed by the time the student transfers to a second institution. Alternatively, some gaps may not be identified until the student transfers and faces new academic situations (e.g., increased writing requirements, greater complexity in content of upper-division courses). Assessing and resolving these deficiencies requires resources that are limited by campus funds and by the availability of developmental education at four-year institutions. Student awareness, motivation, and self-efficacy are crucial to maximizing the use of available services.

Regardless of a student's background and attainment at the previous institution(s), it is common for transfers to struggle academically at their new college. Research has identified the phenomenon of *transfer shock* (Hills, 1965), in which students experience a dip in GPA during their first semester at the four-year institution followed by a recovery in subsequent semesters. Explanations for the dip include adjustments to new academic environment, challenges in personal and social adjustment, new expectations, and lack of transfer-specific resources to address transfer shock (Glass & Harrington, 2002; Laanan, Starobin, & Eggleston, 2010).

Long-held assumptions about student preparedness may contribute to over-generalizing the challenges and underestimating the potential of transfer students. Compared with four-year colleges, two-year colleges enroll a higher proportion of students needing developmental or remedial education (Chen, 2016). It is not uncommon to assume all two-year transfers have the same academic skill set. Misperceptions and generalizations about transfer students' preparedness and lower grades related to transfer shock can blur clarity of students' true abilities.

Navigating a New Institutional Culture

Successfully navigating a new institutional culture, understanding new expectations and roles, and adjusting to new academic standards contribute to persistence and empower students to manage transfer shock and other transition difficulties (Tinto, 2012). Transfer students describe the need to learn a new vernacular, traverse new physical spaces, engage with new activities, identify support, and build new relationships in a short period of time (Flaga, 2006; Laanan, 2001). Examples of these transitions include learning new academic terminology and acronyms, student information systems, and academic processes such as registration. Students may also find that different expectations exist for academic advising and in the classroom. Depending on a student's prior experience, cultural capital, and personal skills and resilience, socially integrating into the new campus is different for each student. Transfer students find themselves immersed in a campus where their peers have already had one to two years to find where they like living, connect with faculty and support services, and explore cocurricular activities.

Increased focus on the distinct nature of the transfer experience has led to more specialized programming and services, such as transfer offices, orientations, and transition seminars. Institutions may want to review the support services, programs, and resources dedicated to transfer support to see whether they align with the number of transfers and the specific needs of those students at their institutions. As with any cohort, the individual student experience is the critical component in student success, and this may be even more relevant for transfer students given the myriad paths that bring them to their current institution. The following sections look at advising strategies to help transfer students as a cohort and as individuals.

Advising Initiatives for Student Success

Considering the challenges discussed above, there are effective approaches for working with individual students, enhancing communication and collaboration on and between campuses, and supporting faculty and professionals who work with transfer students. We can look to campuses for innovative and thoughtful initiatives that address multiple challenges and that provide reasonable and sustainable best practices for everyone working with transfer. Three areas where advising plays a critical role include working directly with students, coordinating with other programs across campus for greater student success, and fostering collaborations between institutions that facilitate more seamless transfer.

Advising Foundations

The individual connections that students make with faculty and staff can contribute to success and persistence while reducing student challenges and anxiety (Laanan, 2007). Effective advising models share common elements, including: listening and developing rapport with students; supporting student decision making and planning; providing accurate information on the college and requirements; referring students to resources; monitoring progress; and providing support for career closure and goal setting. Developmental advising philosophy suggests that "advisors—faculty or staff—focus on educational planning in the context of students' strengths and interests, taking into account their readiness to make solid academic decisions based on their short- and long-term goals" (Grites & Gordon, 2009, p. 14). Consideration should also be given to the ways that advisement initiatives (e.g., individual advising, programs) are assessed and how that assessment evidence is used to inform and improve practices in general and for a specific campus. Additional considerations that can strengthen the philosophy and approach to advising transfer students include the following:

- Acknowledge the unique nature of the transfer student experience and how it differs from the first-year student experience. Validate the challenges of transfer students and demonstrate empathy for those challenges.

- Emphasize the importance of student self-efficacy in understanding curriculum and credit evaluation and how important those are to effective planning and decision making.

- Set expectations for students to build academic plans early on that confirm their career and academic goals, maximize course selection, and address interests in applied learning, such as internships or study abroad. These plans allow transfers to fit these cocurricular options in when possible and establish informed goals for finishing their degree.

- Encourage early and informed self-reflection on academic preparedness and promote student engagement with faculty early in their semester. Students may need support in assessing their academic skills and in anticipating gaps or challenges they may encounter (e.g., writing skills, managing workload). Help students (and faculty) understand that first-semester transfer shock is a common experience and a temporary drop in grades should not be taken as the last word on student potential.

- Recognize that transfer advising may require more time given the unique nature of issues, the need for additional information, and the institutional processes and policies that students must navigate.

The Advising Timeline

The transfer student experience begins well before the student enrolls at their new college. Students are better served when colleges see transfer education as a multi-institution experience and extend services beyond the boundaries of the individual institutions. Advising can contribute to a more seamless journey by addressing key points in an advising timeline that starts before the student enrolls at the new college.

The more information students have on their credit equivalencies and program requirements, the better choices they will make in course planning at all levels of their academic career. Many receiving campuses are bringing advising services to the sending campuses virtually and in-person to create a seamless advising experience. At the University of Arizona, the UA Bridge is a collaboration with several community colleges where students have dedicated UA transfer staff who assist with pre-transfer counseling (http://admissions.arizona.edu/how-to-apply/transfer/ua-bridge). The State University of New York (SUNY) College at Cortland Transfer Mobility Advisor has office space and hours at two community college partner campuses, allowing for an overlap of support from two- to four-year advising. It also serves to increase interaction among the professionals and faculty working with transfer students (http://www2.cortland.edu/transfer-path).

Institutions can consider the following questions to assess advising at every stage of the transfer transition:

Prior to enrollment at new college:

- Do students have access to credit equivalency information while taking courses at their current institution?
- When will credits be evaluated officially?
- How do students access information about their intended transfer major and requirements?

- At what point can students access advisors at the new institution?

- When will direct advising occur for the first time? After acceptance? During orientation?

- When can students register for their first semester at the new institution? There are some indications that earlier course registration of transfer students may lead to greater persistence (Goodman, 2010). Programs, such as the Early Transfer Registration Day at University of Dubuque, are designed to provide academic advising and registration in the semester prior to transfer, which may allay concerns about course availability and foster a greater sense of belonging at the new institution.

Start of the first semester:

- When will advisors be assigned? How does a student find advisor contact information?

- When will the first advising meeting of the semester take place? Who is expected to initiate this meeting?

- When does registration for the upcoming semester occur, and what advising support exists during that time?

- When will the student and advisor confirm an academic plan for completion of the degree? What is the anticipated graduation date, and what is required to meet that goal? Has the student accounted for interest in internships, study abroad, or other academic experiences that affect curricular plans?

Beyond the first semester:

- When will advisors check in on academic progress during the semester (first several weeks; midpoint)?

- Do advisors complete a final grade review at end of first semester? Do they contact advisees with low grades or academic standing issues?

- When is the academic plan reviewed and adjusted as needed based on academic progress, changes in program, or addition of minor or other academic experiences (e.g., study abroad)?

- Have students researched potential career options and articulated how their academic plan resonates with career goals?

- How are students acknowledged for academic achievement—by advisors, deans, or faculty? Is there recognition on campus for successful transfer scholars, such as a campus chapter of Tau Sigma National Honor Society (http://www.tausigmanhs.org/)?

- Has the student become involved with cocurricular activities that engage them in the life of the college? Do they have access to an inventory of academic experiences, such as study abroad, undergraduate research, major clubs, or service-learning? Are they aware of campus activities and organizations that provide ways to connect with other students and expand their personal and social development (e.g., leadership, communication)? Do they have other obligations, such as work, that make this challenging?

- Do advisors take time to ask an advisee how he or she is doing? Using open-ended questions encourages reflection, can provide insight into how students are experiencing college and identify issues an advisor could help with: What is going well and what could be improved? What do they think of the college in general? What questions do they have? What help are they seeking?

Transfer Advising Intake

The first contact with transfer students establishes rapport and is critical for learning about student background, abilities, goals, and concerns. While intake forms or suggestions for initial meetings are important for all advisors, they are especially helpful for working with transfers, as they have a shorter time to become engaged and establish a new academic record. Advisors may be given talking-point suggestions in advisor training or manuals, or they may receive a more formalized template to review with their advisees. These tips are particularly helpful for those advisors who have less experience with transfer students. Sample student questions for an initial intake can range from basic information to more in-depth questions about student goals, preparedness, and motivation.

Basic academic information and planning.

- What prior institutions did you attend, and what major programs did you pursue?

- What questions do you have about the credit review process or how any credits were applied to your program?

- Do you understand the academic program requirements?

- When do you plan to graduate, and do you have an academic plan to meet that timeline?
- What kinds of cocurricular or applied learning experiences (e.g., study abroad, undergraduate research, or internships) interest you? How might they affect your plan?

Academic goals and preparedness.

- In which subjects did you excel at your previous college(s)?
- What subjects were more challenging? Which courses were the most challenging?
- What are your academic goals for this semester (e.g., overall GPA; GPA in major)?
- What academic competencies/skills do you need to build upon in order to be successful (e.g., writing, reading comprehension, quantitative skills, content knowledge)?
- How would you describe your level of preparedness for coursework at this college?
- How confident are you in your study strategies and preparation for tests/assignments?
- How do you manage your academic workload?

Transition and engagement.

- In what activities were you involved at your prior college(s)?
- What clubs or programs are you interested in participating in here?
- Do you plan to work? If so, how many hours do you expect to work each week?
- Do you know other students who attend here?
- Are you living on campus or commuting?
- What did you find interesting about this campus besides your academic program?
- Do you have concerns about finding ways to become involved at this campus?
- How are you feeling about your decision to attend?

Support and resource awareness.

- At your last college, what services did you use to help with your academics (e.g., tutoring services, academic advising)?
- Did you meet with faculty during office hours or participate in study groups?
- Do you have the office hours and contact information for all of your instructors?
- Have you received a list of campus resources, or do you know how to access one?
- What questions do you have about resources on campus?

Expectations for advising.

- What was advising like at your previous institution?
- What do you expect of your academic advisor?
- What do you see as your role in academic advising?

Transfer Credit Evaluation Review

As part of the intake process, a review of transfer credit evaluation can ensure that all possible credits have transferred, clarify how those credits have been applied to the academic program, and address any inconsistencies or concerns the student may have. A checklist for transfer credit evaluation can bring up common questions, ensure that maximum credits are applied to the degree, and avoid registration issues, such as duplicating a course already taken. Advisors and transfer students should review the following regarding transfer evaluation:

- the transfer credit evaluation policies, processes, and relevant contact people/offices;
- how to access the evaluation;
- prior institutions noted on the evaluation;
- student rights and the process to request reevaluation of credits or appeal a decision;
- maximum number of credits transferred according to policy;
- questions about individual course equivalents; and
- questions about how courses apply to the new program (e.g., major, elective, general education).

Transfer Advising as a Specialty

As discussed earlier, the unique nature of the transfer student experience calls for additional advising knowledge and sensitivity. Advising offices and advisors play a significant role in educating campuses about transfer students. Advisors who focus on transfer can increase the quality of service to students and improve college-wide support by educating the campus on transfer experiences and transition, advocating for the transfer perspective in policy making and curriculum development, and presenting evidence that resource allocation for transfer support leads to greater student outcomes. "By raising the profile of transfer students, an institution subtly encourages its agents [faculty and staff] to increase the amount of time, energy, money, and other resources earmarked for the facilitation of transfer student success" (Tobolowsky & Cox, 2012, p. 408).

Campuses have created transfer advising support offices, or initiatives within offices, that assess the needs of transfer students, design outreach specific to those needs, and provide a visible, accessible resource that also symbolizes institutional commitment to these students. Another strategy to expand expertise is offering advisors professional development and materials on topics specific to transfer advising, such as credit evaluation, transfer shock, and transition. Academic departments may identify faculty advisors who are interested in working with transfer students and adjust advising loads in consideration of the additional time that effective transfer advising may require.

In addition to faculty and professional advising, student peers can provide supplemental advising and mentorship. These peers often work at orientations or with transition courses or provide general support through the transfer student's first semester or year. These programs assist with the initial transition and are also shown to support overall student satisfaction with the college experience (Sanchez, Bauer, & Paronto, 2006). Transfer peer programs can be centralized on a campus or specific to academic programs or schools, such as engineering or management, in order to address discipline-specific issues in more depth.

On-Campus Partnerships

"As long as four-year colleges provide the academic and social supports necessary to ease the transition, there is no reason why community college transfers should graduate at lower rates than their junior-level colleagues" (Melguizo, Kienzl, & Alfonso, 2011, p. 270). In recognition of the student experience as a holistic one, advisors and advising offices work with a range of campus colleagues to enhance coordination of services and strengthen advising (Council for the Advancement of Standards in Higher Education, 2015). Institutional services—before, during and after transfer—can enhance student mobility and attainment. Advising leaders can look to campus partners, identify key stakeholders within offices, and review the current, and potential, level of collaboration to improve communication and coordination of services.

Faculty and Curriculum Developers

Advisors can assist faculty as they design and revise curriculum to ensure that the impact on transfer mobility is considered. In addition, advisors can partner with faculty within departments to address the challenges of transfer within certain majors because of curricular requirements and structure. Faculty are the primary source of guidance for clarity in catalog and web information, department-specific advising worksheets and manuals, and in the development and maintenance of degree audit systems. Advising offices can support this work by sharing materials, providing templates, and highlighting best practices among departments.

Admissions

Transfer credit evaluation impacts recruitment and admission of transfers as they look for the best use of their prior credit to shape their college selection. From an advising standpoint, credit evaluation allows students to make academic plans earlier and understand their remaining coursework requirements once matriculated at the new college. The transfer credit evaluation function should be a bridge between admissions and advisement to ensure students receive the most current and accurate information and that professionals and faculty understand the credit evaluation process and policies.

Financial Aid

Financial aid offices are important to advisors, as the increase in cost, change in regulations, and limitations of available aid pose a major challenge for many transfer students. These students are often moving to institutions with higher tuition and fees and possibly incurring additional costs related to relocation and living on campus (Wassmer, Moore, & Shulock, 2004; Zamani, 2004). Additionally, transfer students may be ineligible or less competitive for scholarships because they are not aware of deadlines, do not have established GPAs, and do not have faculty references from the new institution yet (Hood et al., 2009).

Registrar's Offices

Because registrars frequently oversee the functional use of the student information system (e.g., course articulation posting), develop the processes for course registration, and coordinate degree audit systems, they can provide guidance to students as they work directly with academic policies, requirements, and processes. Helping transfer students navigate these processes can give registrars particular insight into issues with applying transfer courses to degrees, challenges related to course scheduling and registration, and misinformation or confusion about academic policies.

Student Affairs and Services

Advisors must have an excellent understanding of the student support systems on a campus in order to encourage student engagement and refer students as appropriate. This includes working with counseling services, tutoring and academic support offices, career services, residence life, multicultural life, health services, and student conduct. It is helpful to educate advisors about these services and appropriate referral protocols as well as educate the service offices on the role of advisors, the scope of their work with students, and how advisement can support holistic student development beyond academics. Emergent advising workshops on mental health, scholarships, and career development demonstrate how advisement increasingly intersects with student development and support services.

Transition Offices and Programs

Depending on campus structure, transition services may be a one-stop office to coordinate all transfer support including orientation, advising, and student services. Conversely, decentralized transition programming may be offered from a range of offices (e.g., residential life, advising, counseling) that work more independently. As transfer needs become clearer, campuses develop transfer orientations that consider students' prior experiences and knowledge along with their unique transitional needs. These orientations address major academic issues and require advisors to assist with those issues.

Another transition strategy being adapted for transfers is an elective or mandatory first-year seminar. The structure of these seminars varies across campuses in terms of credit hours, goals, and delivery. At SUNY Cortland, COR 201: Enhancing the Transfer Experience is designed to emphasize strategies, skills, and resources related to successful transition and academic requirements, policies, and expectations and is taught in the first half of the semester (http://www2.cortland. edu/offices/advisement-and-transition/transfer-students). Stockton University Transfer Seminars are embedded in a content course with faculty who are willing to address transition areas within the context of the course. As part of the campus collaboration expansion, some four-year campuses offer transition seminars on their two-year partner campuses or have developed online courses to start working with students before they transfer.

In addition to orientation and transition seminars, campuses develop individual workshops or series to assist with transitional issues without the time and credit-hour commitment of a seminar. The University of Minnesota-Twin Cities offers the New Transfer Workshop Series of four 75-minute sessions including New to the U and Study Like a Gopher (http://transfer.umn.edu/programs/workshopseries/index.html). If not already involved with transition programs, advisors can partner with colleagues coordinating these programs to discuss how academic planning and decision making may fit into the programming and assess the ways advising is addressed within the entire context of a campus's transition services for transfers.

Inter-Campus Collaborations

In addition to collaborating with colleagues on campus, advisors have a role in enhancing collaboration with other colleges, especially with respect to conversations about curriculum. State systems have established transfer initiatives that are designed to create multi-campus course articulations and transfer paths and provide tools, such as shared degree audit systems, for students to understand how credits will apply. The University of Texas at Austin Transfer Resources link students to an automated transfer equivalency system with a database of more than 300,000 credit evaluations and an interactive degree audit that estimates how courses will transfer to a new degree. This includes transfer paths within disciplines representing core requirements identified through faculty discussions at two- and four-year colleges. The State University of New York Transfer Paths identify lower division requirements that all SUNY campuses should offer for specific majors or disciplines to ensure transferring students have completed foundational coursework and can move into higher level requirements upon transfer.

Articulation agreements between campuses create a shared understanding of the relationship between programs and courses from one campus to another. Advisors need to be informed about existing agreements and have access to course or program articulations. Colleges may also form multi-institution consortia based on region or enrollment patterns. This allows campuses to have focused discussions to clarify student learning outcomes and equivalencies at program and course levels, share curricular changes affecting transfer students, identify and respond to challenges that students encounter in navigating multiple curricula, and create shared resources. At SUNY Cortland, the Advisement and Transition office worked with academic departments on campus and at community colleges to create a transfer planning sheet for each academic major. The planning sheet highlights courses that should be taken at the community colleges before enrolling at SUNY Cortland for the best academic plan.

The advisor's role in curricular communication starts with being a part of articulation and policy development discussions, as they have first-hand knowledge of how students experience an academic program. Advisors should advocate to be part of planning discussions and intercampus meetings and serve as key stakeholders in evaluating potential tools to ensure that the advisee perspective is fully considered. This engagement will also help advisors to better educate and support students in their understanding of policies and use of systems and tools. When needed, advisors can help establish and facilitate communication by creating venues for dialogue to engage professionals and faculty from partner institutions.

Conclusion

Additional information on advising and transfer can by explored by visiting NACADA: The Global Academic Advising Community, the National Resource Center for The First-Year Experience and Students in Transition, and resources provided in the chapter Appendix. Research on transfer and sharing of best practices from the field will create deeper understanding among faculty and staff, campus leadership, and broader system leadership regarding what transfers bring to campuses and how to help them succeed.

Effective advisement addresses significant challenges of transfer, offers critical support to students, and contributes to greater student achievement. Institutions can better serve these students by establishing advising approaches that acknowledge the unique nature of the transfer experience, the particular needs of these students, and the standards and requirements for quality advisement. Cooperation among service offices within a campus and collaboration among institutions that send and receive transfer students are key to building shared understanding and systems for more seamless transfer.

Advisors can be a consistent, accessible source of information and support, helping transfer students manage the complexities of the curriculum, establish meaningful goals and plans, and navigate a new culture including its systems, rules, and expectations. Throughout the advisement process, advisors also assist students in developing the communication and problem-solving skills to make them confident and resourceful agents in their academic experience. Whether it is helping the individual student or advocating for all transfer students, advising has a meaningful role in the shared success of students and institutions.

References

Bowen, W. G., Chingos, M. M., & McPherson, M. S. (2009). *Crossing the finish line: Completing college at America's public universities.* Princeton, NJ: Princeton University Press.

Chen, X. (2016). *Remedial coursetaking at US public 2- and 4-year institutions: Scope, experiences, and outcomes* (NCES 2016-405). U.S. Department of Education. Washington, DC: National Center for Education Statistics.

Council for the Advancement of Standards in Higher Education. (2015). *CAS professional standards for higher education* (9th ed.). Washington, DC.

Doyle, W. R. (2006, May/June). Community college transfers and college graduation: Whose choices matter most? *Change,* 55-59.

Drake, J. K. (2011). The role of academic advising in student retention and persistence. *About Campus, 16*(3), 8-12.

Eggleston, L. E., & Laanan, F. S. (2001, Summer). Making the transition to the senior institution. *New Directions for Community Colleges,* 87-97.

Flaga, C. T. (2006). The process of transition for community college transfer students. *Community College Journal of Research and Practice, 30*(1), 3-19.

Glass, J. C., & Harrington, A. R. (2002). Academic performance of community college transfer students and 'native' students at a large state university. *Journal of Research and Practice, 26,* 415-430.

Goodman, P. A. (2010). *Predictors of persistence for first-time, full-time community and technical college students* (Doctoral dissertation). Walden University, Minneapolis, Minnesota.

Grites, T. & Gordon, V. N. (2009, Spring). Developmental academic advising revisited. *NACADA Journal, 29,* 119-122.

Hagedorn, L., Serra, M., Hye, S., Cypers, S., Maxwell, W. E., & Lester, J. (2006). Transfer between community colleges and four-year colleges: The all-American game. *Community College Journal of Research and Practice, 30,* 223-242.

Hills, J. R. (1965). Transfer shock: The academic performance of the junior college transfer. *Journal of Experimental Education, 33*(3), 201-215.

Hood, L., Hunt, E., & Haeffele, L. (2009). Illinois post-secondary transfer students: Experiences in navigating the higher education transfer system. *Planning and Changing, 39*(2), 12-19.

Ishitani, T. (2008). How do transfers survive after transfer shock? A longitudinal study of transfer student departure at a four-year institution. *Research in Higher Education, 49*(5), 403-419.

Laanan, F. S. (2001). Transfer student adjustment. *New Directions for Community Colleges, 114,* 5-14.

Laanan, F. S. (2007). Studying transfer students: Part II: Dimensions of transfer students' adjustments. *Community College Journal of Research and Practice, 31,* 37-59.

Laanan, F. S., Starobin, S. S., & Eggleston, L. E. (2010). Adjustment of community college students at a four-year university: Role and relevance of transfer student capital for student retention. *Journal of College Student Retention: Research, Theory & Practice, 12*(2), 175–209.

Lumina Foundation for Education. (2009, February). *A stronger nation through higher education: How and why Americans must meet a big goal for attainment.* Indianapolis, IN.

Marling, J. L. (2013). Navigating the new normal: Transfer trends, issues, and recommendations. *New Directions for Higher Education, 162,* 77-87.

McGuire, S. P., & Belcheir, M. (2013). Transfer student characteristics matter. *Journal of College Student Retention: Research, Theory & Practice, 15*(1), 37–48.

Melguizo, T., Kienzl, G., & Alfonso, M. (2011). Comparing the educational attainment of community college transfer students and four-year rising juniors using propensity score matching. *The Journal of Higher Education, 82*(3), 265-291.

Pascarella, E. T., & Terenzini, P. T. (2005). *How college affects students: A third decade of research.* San Francisco, CA: Jossey-Bass.

Roksa, J., & Calcagno, J. (2008). *Making the transition to four-year institutions: Academic preparation and transfer* (Working Paper No. 13). New York, NY: Community College Research Center, Teachers College, Columbia University. Retrieved from https://ccrc.tc.columbia.edu/publications/transition-to-four-year-institutions.html

Sanchez, R. J., Bauer, T. N., & Paronto, M. E. (2006). Peer-mentoring freshmen: Implications for satisfaction, commitment and retention to graduation. *Academy of Management Learning & Education, 5*(1), 25-37.

Simone, S. A. (2014). *Transferability of postsecondary credit following student transfer or coenrollment* (NCES 2014-163). Washington, DC: National Center for Education Statistics, U.S. Department of Education.

Tinto, V. (2012). *Completing college: Rethinking institutional action.* Chicago, IL: University of Chicago Press.

Tobolowsky, B., & Cox, B. (2012). Rationalizing neglect: An institutional response to transfer students. *The Journal of Higher Education, 83*(3), 389-410.

Wang, X. (2012). Factors contributing to the upward transfer of baccalaureate aspirants beginning at community colleges. *The Journal of Higher Education, 83*(6), 851-875.

Wassmer, R., Moore, C., & Shulock, N. (2004). The effect of racial/ethnic composition on transfer rates in community colleges: Implications for policy and practice. *Research in Higher Education, 45*(6), 651-672.

Zamani, E. M. (2004, Summer). Institutional responses to barrier to the transfer process. *New Directions for Community Colleges, 114,* 15-24.

APPENDIX

ADDITIONAL RESOURCES FOR TRANSFER ADVISING

Organizations

NACADA: The Global Community for Academic Advising
www.nacada.ksu.edu

National Institute for the Study of Transfer Students
www.nists.org

National Resource Center for The First-Year Experience and Students in Transition
www.sc.edu/fye

Selected Publications

Journals

Academic Advising Today
Journal of Academic Advising (Indiana University)
Journal of The First-Year Experience & Students in Transition
The Mentor (Penn State Division of Undergraduate Studies)
NACADA Journal

Books

Drake, J. K., Jordan, P., & Miller, M. A. (Eds.). (2013). *Academic advising approaches: Strategies that teach students to make the most of college.* Manhattan, KS: National Academic Advising Association.

Handel, S. J., & Strempel, E. (Eds.). (2014). *Transition and transformation: Fostering transfer student success.* Dahlonega, GA: University of North Georgia, National Institute for the Study of Transfer Students.

CHAPTER 6

LONG-TERM LEARNING COMMUNITIES: MITIGATING THE EFFECTS OF STEREOTYPE THREAT AND CULTIVATING STUDENT SUCCESS

Kathleen Plinske

Stereotype threat, "the phenomenon whereby individuals perform more poorly on a task when a relevant stereotype or stigmatized social identity is made salient in the performance situation" (Schmader & Johns, 2003, p. 440), has repeatedly been shown to adversely affect students' academic performance. In fact, stereotype threat has been found to contribute to underperformance on a range of diverse tasks, including women's performance in math (Spencer, Steele, & Quinn, 1998) as well as African American, Hispanic, and immigrant students' performance on standardized tests (Chateignier, Dutrévis, Nugier, & Chekroun, 2009; Rodriguez, 2014; Steele & Aronson, 1995). Indeed, "the threat of being viewed through the lens of a negative stereotype, or the fear of doing something that would inadvertently confirm that stereotype" (Steele, 1999, p. 46), can significantly undermine academic performance.

On the campus of a community college with students who predominantly come from underserved backgrounds, the risk of stereotype threat is high. First-generation students may wonder if they are "college material," English language learners may doubt their ability to communicate effectively, and immigrant students may question if they belong. This type of uncertainty, or the sense that "people like me do not belong here," can undermine students' motivation and performance (Walton & Cohen, 2007, p. 83).

Fortunately, research also has revealed that it is possible to mitigate the effects of stereotype threat. Indeed, "it is possible to create niches in which negative stereotypes are not felt to apply. In specific classrooms, within specific programs, even in the climate of entire schools, it is possible to weaken a group's sense of being threatened" (Steele, 1999, p. 54). One powerful way to reduce the effect of stereotype threat is to increase students' sense of belonging (Thoman, Smith, Brown, Chase, & Lee, 2013). Faculty and staff at Valencia College's Osceola Campus have created a number of cohort programs structured as learning communities to foster students' sense of belonging and increase the likelihood of their success. These cohort programs have demonstrated tremendous promise, closing gaps in student performance and significantly increasing students' persistence and academic momentum.

Valencia College

Valencia College (Valencia) is a community college with campuses in both Orange and Osceola counties in Florida, serving more than 60,000 students each year in the greater Orlando area. Along with a handful of other local community colleges, Valencia enjoys a special partnership with the University of Central Florida (UCF) called DirectConnect to UCF (DirectConnect). DirectConnect guarantees admission to UCF to any student who completes an Associate in Arts degree; the pathway is so successful that nearly one quarter of UCF graduates transferred to UCF from Valencia (UCF Office of Institutional Research, 2016). As with any community college, Valencia plays a critical role in providing access to higher education; however, the DirectConnect partnership positions Valencia uniquely in the central Florida education ecosystem to also provide access to baccalaureate-level educational programs.

Creating Access to Higher Education in Osceola County

Valencia's role in providing access to higher education is of utmost importance in Osceola County, which has historically had one of the lowest college-going rates in the state of Florida. In fact, in 2010, Osceola County ranked 61st out of 67 counties in the state in terms of the percentage (40.1%) of high school graduates who enrolled in a public postsecondary institution (Florida Department of Education, 2017). Moreover, the educational attainment level of adults in Osceola County is relatively low. In 2012, only 25% of adults in Osceola County held an associate degree or higher compared with 33% of adults statewide (U.S. Census Bureau, 2013). This combination of facts is especially troubling given the importance of postsecondary education in today's economy. A recent study by Georgetown University revealed that of the 11.6 million jobs created nationally since the depths of the recession in 2008, only 80,000 of them were filled by individuals with only a high school diploma (Carnevale, Jayasundera, & Gulish, 2016). As such, for the future of Osceola County, it became obvious that there was an economic, social, and moral imperative to increase the county's college-going rate.

Valencia's Osceola Campus serves as the primary point of access to higher education in Osceola County. Serving more than 19,000 students annually, the student body of the campus is nearly 50% Hispanic and more than 10% African American, closely reflecting the diversity of its surrounding community. Enrollment at the campus increased more than 10% between 2010 and 2016 (Valencia

College Institutional Research, 2017a), largely due to the 20% increase in Osceola County's college-going rate during the same timeframe (Florida Department of Education, 2017). Of all of the high school graduates in Osceola County who attend college, nearly 75% attend Valencia (Florida Department of Education, 2017; Valencia College Institutional Research, 2016).

While creating greater access to higher education is an important first step, it is not enough as a stand-alone strategy. After all, enrolling in college without completing a credential is certainly not a predictor of future economic prosperity and may even exacerbate future financial woes (Huelsman, 2015). As such, faculty and staff at Valencia were just as interested in strategies to improve student learning outcomes and success as they were in increasing the number of students enrolling in college.

At the invitation of the Lumina Foundation in 2004, Valencia joined Achieving the Dream (AtD), a reform network that champions evidence-based institutional change to improve success results for all students, especially low-income students and students of color. As a result of Valencia's work with AtD, the college created a data team that closely examined student success rates, student persistence, and differences in student performance disaggregated by ethnicity, gender, and level of preparation for college. The data team structured and convened college-wide conversations and reflection on student performance that directly informed the college's strategic plan.

One of the goals of Valencia's 2008-2013 strategic plan was Learning Assured, which had as an outcome to "establish learning and learning support systems and techniques designed to reduce achievement gaps among groups of learners from diverse backgrounds" (Valencia College, 2008). One of the most noticeable gaps in achievement among students at Valencia was observed between students with varying levels of preparation for college. Considering only first-time-in-college degree-seeking students enrolling in Fall 2004, Valencia's three-year graduation rate for students who did not require any developmental coursework was 28%, while the three-year graduation rate for students who required developmental coursework in reading, writing, and mathematics was only 4%. This gap only widened when considering five-year graduation rates: 44% of college-ready students graduated within five years, while only 11% of students requiring developmental coursework in all three areas did (Valencia College Institutional Research, 2017b).

Faculty and staff were deeply concerned about these achievement gaps and the likelihood of a student graduating who required developmental coursework in all three areas, particularly given that approximately 20% of degree-seeking students who enrolled at Valencia fit in this category (Valencia College Institutional

Research, 2017b). Faculty even debated the ethics of admitting and accepting tuition dollars from students with such deficiencies in college preparedness, given the relatively small likelihood of them having a successful outcome. Nevertheless, committed to the college's mission of open access, a team of faculty and staff wanted to explore whether the creation of a robust, long-term learning community for students requiring developmental coursework in all three areas could improve student outcomes and close performance gaps.

Learning Communities and Cohort Programs

Learning communities are hardly a recent educational innovation. In fact, in a 1984 report, the National Institute of Education recommended that every college and university create learning communities (p. 33). In the 1990s, learning communities proliferated at community colleges and universities (Minkier, 2002), and by 2000, more than 500 institutions had established learning communities (Fink & Inkelas, 2015).

Learning communities are often characterized by a group of courses that are linked together, so that all students in the learning community take the same group of courses together, or by a restructuring of the curriculum altogether. This grouping or restructuring encourages students to develop a deeper and integrated understanding of the course material (Gabelnick, MacGregor, Matthews, & Smith, 1990, p. 19). Recognized as a high-impact educational practice (Kuh, 2008), "learning communities and use of collaborative pedagogies that require students to learn together in a coherent, interdependent manner leads to higher levels of academic and social engagement, greater rates of course completion, and higher rates of persistence" (Engstrom & Tinto, 2007, p. 3).

Further, learning communities that have been designed for underserved student populations have been found to foster students' relationships with one another and to help students feel a sense of belonging (Fink & Hummel, 2015, p. 33). Interventions to increase students' sense of belonging have been found to reduce stereotype threat and increase student persistence and academic performance (Hausmann, Ye, Schofield, & Woods, 2009; Walton & Cohen, 2007).

While the majority of learning communities at community colleges last one semester (Hatch & Bohlig, 2015), Valencia's Osceola Campus has designed and implemented a number of long-term learning community experiences that last multiple semesters, or even multiple years. These are described in the sections that follow.

REACH

In 2011, the Osceola Campus piloted a learning community program specifically for students requiring developmental coursework in all three areas (reading, writing, and mathematics). The program, called REACH, was designed such that students enrolled in their first three semesters in college (fall, spring, and summer) in a structured learning community with a predetermined course schedule. Students did not choose the courses in which they would enroll, nor their specific course sections; rather, students who registered for REACH were assigned the days and times their classes would meet during their first three semesters in college and were enrolled in pre-selected courses.

In the fall term, students were enrolled in Beginning Algebra (developmental mathematics), Developmental Writing II, Developmental Reading II, and Student Success, for a total of 12 semester credit hours. In the spring term, students enrolled in Freshman Composition I, Intermediate Algebra, Fundamentals of Speech, and Introduction to Humanities, again for a total of 12 semester credit hours. In the summer term, students enrolled in Freshman Composition II and College Algebra for a total of six semester credit hours. Whereas many students who are placed into developmental coursework ultimately never even enroll in college-level courses (Bailey & Cho, 2010), students who successfully completed the REACH program earned 21 college-level credits (30 total credit hours) by the conclusion of their first academic year, a significant milestone of academic progress and momentum.

In addition to the structured course schedule, students in the REACH program are required to participate in cocurricular activities designed and facilitated by REACH faculty. These activities are intended to build students' awareness of resources available at the college, develop their resilience in the face of adversity, and help them make the transition to college-level coursework and make personal connections at the college.

Faculty members who teach in the REACH program meet on a regular basis to discuss student performance and concerns. They share observations about student attendance and engagement and strategically develop interventions for students who appear to be struggling. This approach serves as an effective and personalized early-alert system starting the first week of the semester. Moreover, faculty collaborate on integrated assignments and course sequencing and assignment due dates to create a coherent learning experience for students in the program.

The REACH program has enrolled new students every fall term at the Osceola Campus since 2011. Prior to 2014, potential REACH students were identified by their college placement scores and were recruited during New Student Orientation. However, the Florida legislature passed a bill that no longer allowed colleges to require that students complete a college readiness test nor mandate that students enroll in developmental education coursework. Accordingly, it became more diffi-cult to (a) identify students who could benefit from the program and (b) encourage students to enroll in developmental education coursework that was now optional. Faculty and student affairs staff members at the Osceola Campus collaborate with local high school guidance counselors and college transition coaches to identify students who, based on their performance in high school, are ideal candidates for the REACH program. Further, the college offers a $500 scholarship as an incentive to enroll in the program. At its peak, prior to 2014, the REACH program enrolled 100 students per year. Currently, with the changes in developmental education in Florida, the REACH program enrolls about 25 students per year.

Students who have participated in REACH have outperformed their peers with similar levels of preparedness for college on measures that are leading indi-cators of a student's likelihood to graduate. While fewer than half of the students requiring developmental coursework in reading, writing, and mathematics histor-ically persisted into their second year at Valencia, students who have participated in REACH have had a fall-to-fall persistence rate of 70%. Moreover, while fewer than one third of students requiring developmental coursework in all three areas historically completed 15 credit hours in two years, 71% of students in REACH have achieved this important milestone of academic progress. In fact, the levels of persistence and academic progress for students who participate in REACH have mirrored the success rates of students who arrive at Valencia without requiring any remediation.

Camino a UCF

Based on the success of the REACH program, faculty and staff at the Osce-ola Campus were interested in the possibility of designing a cohort program for students arriving at Valencia who were prepared for college-level coursework. Moreover, faculty and staff wondered whether a cohort model could be successful across the entire length of an associate degree program, rather than just a student's first academic year.

In 2014, Valencia and UCF were invited to participate in the Engaging Latino Students for Transfer and College Completion Institute organized by the National Survey of Student Engagement and the Center for Community College Student Engagement. One of the goals of the institute was to build awareness and consid-eration of factors that may inhibit or enhance student engagement, persistence, transfer, and completion for Latino students, leading to the development of a concrete action plan to increase Latino student transfer and success rates.

In an effort to achieve the greatest impact, Valencia and UCF agreed to collaborate on an initiative to support students choosing two of the most popular majors for transfers: business and psychology. The goal was to design a program that would support students through successful completion of an Associate in Arts degree while preparing them for transfer to UCF in their intended field of study and to help reduce the effects of transfer shock, which can result in an appreciable drop in students' grades in the first semester after transfer from a community college to a university (Hills, 1965).

As part of the design process, faculty and staff from Valencia and UCF examined students' historical enrollment patterns and course success data. The data revealed that many Valencia transfer students were not completing second-year courses that are required as part of their major prior to transfer and struggled when they enrolled in those courses at UCF. For example, 29% of Valencia transfer students who enrolled in Principles of Microeconomics (ECO 2023) at UCF were unsuccessful in their first attempt, and 47% of transfers who enrolled in Statistical Methods (STA 2023) at UCF did not successfully complete it on their first attempt (UCF Office of Operational Excellence and Assessment Support, 2014). Nevertheless, ECO 2023 is required for business majors and STA 2023 is required for psychology majors, and both are offered at Valencia. It was unclear why students were choosing not to complete those courses before transferring to the university. Similarly, many of the junior- and senior-level courses required of business and psychology majors at UCF are offered via distance learning, and the data revealed that Valencia transfer students were not as successful in courses offered via distance learning as students who enrolled at UCF as first-time-in-college students.

Accordingly, a two-year cohort program called Camino a Una Comunidad Fuerte (UCF) was designed that included all of the first- and second-year program prerequisites for UCF's baccalaureate programs in business or psychology. Hybrid courses are scheduled in the first year of the program, with fully online courses included in the second year, to prepare students to be successful in distance-learning modalities at UCF. The program is designed such that students enroll in 15 credit hours each fall and spring term, a credit load that is correlated with higher graduation rates at UCF. When students enroll in Camino a UCF, they agree to a predetermined course schedule (Tuesday and Thursday afternoons and Friday mornings), while their major determines the specific courses in which they enroll. Built into the schedule is an Activity Hour on Tuesdays and Thursdays during which no classes are scheduled. During that time, students are expected to participate in meaningful cocurricular activities, many of which are collaboratively offered by Valencia and UCF, such as faculty guest lectures and advising sessions.

In addition, Valencia students in the Camino a UCF program have the opportunity to participate in UCF student activities. For example, students can participate in Spirit Splash (UCF's homecoming event), attend a football and basketball game, and have their photo taken with Knightro, UCF's mascot. These activities allow students to feel part of UCF before they actually transfer.

Students who participate in Camino a UCF complete their associate degrees at a much faster rate than average. Of the 44 students who enrolled in the first Camino a UCF cohort in Fall 2015, 16 had completed their associate degrees by Spring 2017. While Valencia's five-year graduation rate for all degree-seeking students has reached 35% (Valencia College Institutional Research, 2017b), a higher percentage of students enrolled in the first Camino a UCF cohort graduated in only two years.

Future Teachers Academy

While the powerful value proposition of DirectConnect is a guarantee of admission to UCF upon completion of an associate degree, several faculty and staff at the Osceola Campus wondered whether it was possible to create a value proposition beyond students' completion of a baccalaureate degree. In other words, was it possible to build a 2+2+career partnership, where after graduating from UCF, students were guaranteed employment in their field of study?

The School District of Osceola County (SDOC), like many school districts in Central Florida, is experiencing a critical teacher shortage. For the 2016-2017 school year, there were approximately 650 teaching vacancies within the SDOC (Russon, 2017). Moreover, the state of Florida prepares less than 4% of its teachers, relying on recruiting and hiring teachers from other states (Sutcher, Darling-Hammond, & Carver-Thomas, 2016, p. 30), which can cause school districts to compete for out-of-state talent. The SDOC approached the Osceola Campus with a request: Would it be possible to grow our own teachers?

The Future Teachers Academy is designed as a four-year cohort program for Osceola Campus students interested in a career in teaching. In the first two years of the program, students will earn an Associate in Arts degree from Valencia while completing all the program prerequisites for a bachelor's degree in elementary education at UCF. Upon completion of their associate degrees, students will transfer via DirectConnect and complete their bachelor's in elementary education. By agreement with UCF and the SDOC, students will complete their classroom observations, internships, and student teaching at schools within the SDOC. Upon completing their bachelor's degrees, students are guaranteed a job offer with the SDOC.

Students who participate in the program agree to a course schedule that meets on Tuesdays, Wednesdays, and Thursdays, allowing them to serve as substitute teachers with the SDOC on Mondays and Fridays. This detail of the program schedule helps the SDOC meet its need to find qualified substitute teachers on the days of the week when there is highest demand and also provides students with meaningful professional development experience and part-time employment.

Student participants receive tuition scholarships throughout the program. The Central Florida Educators Federal Credit Union made a charitable contribution allowing for a $1,000 scholarship for each student participant. The scholarship is awarded in $200 increments each semester during the first two years of the program upon successful completion of all program requirements in the previous term. The SDOC has committed to paying a $2,500 stipend to each of the participants during the third and fourth year of the program to help offset university tuition costs.

Staying true to the original design of Osceola County growing its own teachers, students were recruited for the program from the county's graduating high school seniors. The first cohort, launched in Fall 2017, was filled to capacity before the student participants had even graduated from high school. While it will be several years before success of the program can be assessed, it certainly seems to be off to a promising start.

Challenges

While the benefits of creating learning communities and cohort programs are significant, so too can be the challenges. However, being aware of potential challenges and planning for them in advance can mitigate their effects.

Program Recruitment

One significant challenge that can threaten the viability of a well-designed cohort program is difficulty in recruiting students. The value proposition to students as a result of their participation in the program must be clear. Recruiting students into a cohort program requires them to agree to a specific course schedule, which may not be ideal for them based on their work and family obligations. Cohort programs also require students to enroll in a certain number of credit hours, which may represent a heavier course load than the students had planned. Moreover, cohort programs require students to give up the ability to select individual professors based on peer recommendations or popularity ratings such as *Rate My Professor*. In a sense, inviting students to participate in a cohort program requires asking them to give up control over certain essential elements of their college experience. Students will want to know, "What's in it for me?"

Trying to convince students to join a cohort program because they will have a better chance of graduating is not a clear enough value proposition. Instead, the essential elements of the program that take place outside the classroom can serve as a powerful recruiting tool. Highlighting the cocurricular activities (e.g., field trips, guest speakers, field experiences) that students in the program will have exclusive access to can serve as a powerful incentive. A small scholarship can also serve as a clear incentive for participation. Further, unique access to partner organizations upon completion of the program (e.g., guaranteed admission to a partner university, guaranteed employment) also represent powerful value propositions to potential students.

Hyperbonding and Peer Fatigue

Ironically, the more successful a cohort program is, the more challenging it can become over time, particularly for instructors. When students enroll in courses with a peer group over multiple semesters, or even across multiple years, they can become very close, and occasionally *hyperbond* (Watts, 2013). When a new semester begins, instructors who have not yet taught in the cohort can feel, and be treated, like outsiders. Classroom management can be a significant challenge for instructors when students feel very close to one another and when they feel ownership for the cohort.

On the contrary, students who participate in a cohort program may suffer from peer fatigue, in which they grow tired of some of their classmates and wish for the opportunity to take classes with students outside the cohort. This commonly happens when students with strong personalities enroll in a cohort. Students who experience peer fatigue may request to opt out of the cohort just to escape certain classmates with whom they have grown frustrated or annoyed.

One strategy to prevent both hyperbonding and peer fatigue is to create a cohort that is larger than the capacity of individual course sections. In other words, if the courses in the cohort program have a capacity of 25-30 students, it is a good idea to enroll at least 50-60 students in the cohort program. This allows for the creation of a learning community among the larger group while allowing for rotation of students within individual courses across semesters. If enrolling a large cohort is not possible, another strategy is to limit participation to a number of students that is smaller than the capacity of individual courses and allow students not part of the cohort program to fill the rest of the seats in the course. Either strategy allows for variety in course rosters across semesters, important to preventing (or responding to) hyperbonding and peer fatigue.

Stepping Out of Sequence

No matter how carefully a cohort program is planned, students will undoubtedly experience varying levels of success. Even in the strongest cohorts, it is likely that at least one student will not successfully complete all the courses required in a given semester. When a student falls out of step with the rest of her cohort, challenging questions arise: How should the student make up the course? Should the student be allowed to continue in the rest of the course sequence with the other members of her cohort?

Exacerbating this challenge are the relationships among students in the cohort. If the student is not allowed to continue in the program, other students may rally behind her and lobby for her re-admission. If a different student was not allowed to continue in the program in a previous semester, but this student is allowed to do so, some students might think the other student was treated unfairly.

There are no simple solutions to this challenge. In fact, efforts to write a catch-all policy that allows for a certain number of unsuccessful course attempts before a student is not allowed to continue in the program, or creating a one-strike rule, can be counterproductive, leading to decisions that are not in the best interests of students based on individual circumstances. For example, a student who does not successfully complete a course that is a prerequisite to a required course in the following semester faces a more significant challenge than one who does not successfully complete an elective course that could be retaken in a subsequent term without significantly impeding academic progress.

Instead, the college should have a thoughtful plan about how to respond when a student falls out of step with the cohort, and a process by which a decision will be made regarding continued participation in the program. It is also helpful to identify the specific criteria that will be used to consider whether the student should continue. The college should clearly communicate with students at the beginning of the program about what happens when a student does not successfully complete all of the required courses in a given semester, including sharing that each student's situation will be assessed individually. It is also helpful to consider the college's existing academic grievance policies, and whether a student would be able to use an existing process to appeal a decision about continued participation in the program, or if a different appeal mechanism should be created. It is important that each of these steps are in place well before a decision needs to be made about a student's continued participation in the program, and not developed on the fly.

Characteristics of Successful Cohort Programs

Through the creation and implementation of these highly structured cohort programs, several common characteristics emerged that appear to be critically important to the programs' success.

Faculty Participation Outside the Classroom

The success of cohort programs depends on faculty involvement, including the organization of and participation in cocurricular activities, as well as engaging in discussions with other faculty members about student performance on a regular basis. It may be helpful to formalize the expectations for faculty participation that are outside the normal scope of classroom duties and to make faculty aware of these expectations during program recruitment. Formally recognizing each faculty member's participation in the program, which could take the form of a stipend, a reassignment of teaching duties, or recognition of service to the college, can help ensure that faculty are not caught off guard by additional expectations for involvement with students. For example, faculty who engage deeply in one of the cohort programs at the Osceola Campus fulfill their expectations of service to the college and are, therefore, typically relieved of expectations to serve on college-wide committees.

Administrative Leadership

Developing a multi-semester or multi-year cohort program requires significant coordination across multiple academic divisions. It is helpful to assign an administrative leader, usually a dean, to be responsible for ensuring that course schedules are developed with proper faculty assignments to fulfill the design of the program. Usually this means coordinating with deans in other academic areas to develop the course schedule at least one year in advance. Moreover, this requires a tremendous degree of collaboration and communication within the academic leadership team. For cohort programs to succeed, individual academic divisions cannot operate in silos nor create their course schedules in a vacuum.

The academic leader responsible for the cohort program should also be willing to lead discussions about recruitment strategies and be skilled at collaborating with others across the college and outside the institution to recruit student participants. For example, recruitment for cohort programs can be a successful strategy in new student orientation, but only if orientation staff are aware of the program and supportive of recruiting students. Similarly, local high school guidance counselors and transition coaches can be essential in identifying ideal student participants for the program, but only if they understand the value for their students. The administrator responsible for the program should play a pivotal role in building these essential collaborative relationships.

Moreover, the academic leader should convene regular meetings of the faculty involved in the program. These meetings can facilitate conversations about student performance, creating an informal early-alert system while also serving as an opportunity to identify potential program improvement. The academic leader can use such input to implement changes at the programmatic level.

Partnership with Student Affairs

A successful cohort program depends on a strong partnership with the campus's student affairs team. Advising staff members, who often have a wealth of experience working with students to select courses, can provide important insights regarding the sequence in which courses (for which there are not formal prerequisites) should be taken and courses for which concurrent enrollment in the same semester are recommended. In addition, advisors and orientation staff can share important feedback about what course schedules would likely be most attractive to students based on their experiences working with students and observing their preferences. Transfer advisors can also help identify changes in program prerequisites at the university level that would necessitate a redesign of the cohort program.

A successful cohort feels like a holistically coordinated learning experience for students. This feeling is only possible when student affairs is a partner in the work and student services are deeply integrated into the program.

Conclusion

Long-term cohort programs help to create a coherent educational experience for students. Moreover, the structured design of these programs reduces curricular complexity and accelerates students' academic momentum. While they require significant coordination and planning, long-term cohort programs are characterized by a deep sense of community. Students who feel a sense of social connectedness and belonging on campus are less likely to experience the effects of stereotype threat and more likely to persist and succeed in college. As such, we owe it to our students and our communities to create conditions that best support student learning and eliminate any doubt that students may have about whether they belong on campus.

References

Bailey, T., & Cho, S. W. (2010). *Developmental education in community colleges* [Issue Brief]. New York, NY: Community College Research Center, Teachers College, Columbia University.

Carnevale, A. P., Jayasundera, T., & Gulish, A. (2016). *America's divided recovery: College haves and have-nots.* Washington, DC: Georgetown University Center on Education and the Workforce.

Chateignier, C., Dutrévis, M., Nugier, A., & Chekroun, P. (2009). French-Arab students and verbal intellectual performance: Do they really suffer from a negative intellectual stereotype? *European Journal of Psychology of Education, 24*(2), 219-234.

Engstrom, C., & Tinto, V. (2007). *Pathways to student success: The impact of learning communities on the success of academically under-prepared college students.* Final report prepared for the William and Flora Hewlett Foundation.

Fink, J. E., & Hummel, M. L. (2015). With educational benefits for all: Campus inclusion through learning communities designed for underserved populations. In M. Benjamin (Ed.), *Learning communities from start to finish* (New Directions for Student Services, No. 149, pp. 29-40). San Francisco, CA: Jossey-Bass.

Fink, J. E., & Inkelas, K. K. (2015). A history of learning communities within American higher education. In M. Benjamin (Ed.), *Learning communities from start to finish* (New Directions for Student Services, No. 149, pp. 5-11). San Francisco, CA: Jossey-Bass.

Florida Department of Education. (2017). *High school feedback report: 2010 Florida public high school graduates district comparison* [Data File]. Retrieved from http://data.fldoe.org/readiness/

Gabelnick, F., MacGregor, J., Matthews, R., & Smith, B. L. (1990). *Learning communities: Creating connections among students, faculty, and disciplines.* San Francisco, CA: Jossey-Bass.

Hatch, D. K., & Bohlig, M. (2015). The score and design of structured group learning experiences at community colleges. *Community College Journal of Research and Practice, 39*(9), 819-838.

Hausmann, L. R. M., Ye, F., Schofield, J. W., & Woods, R. L. (2009). Sense of belonging and persistence in White and African-American first-year students. *Research in Higher Education, 50*(7), 649-669.

Hills, J. (1965). Transfer shock: The academic performance of the transfer student. *The Journal of Experimental Education, 33*(3). (ERIC Document Reproduction Service No. ED 010 740)

Huelsman, M. (2015). *The debt divide: The racial and class bias behind the "new normal" of student borrowing.* New York, NY: Demos.

Kuh, G. D. (2008). *High-impact educational practices: What they are, who has access to them, and why they matter.* Washington, DC: Association of American Colleges and Universities.

Minkier, J. E. (2002). ERIC review: Learning communities at the community college. *Community College Review, 30*(3), 31-45.

National Institute of Education. (1984). *Involvement in learning: Realizing the potential of American higher education. Final report of the study group on the conditions of excellence in American Higher Education.* (Stock No. 065-000-00213-2). Washington, DC: U.S. Government Printing Office.

Rodríguez, B. A. (2014). The threat of living up to expectations: Analyzing the performance of Hispanic students on standardized exams. *Journal of Hispanic Higher Education, 13*(3), 191-205.

Russon, G. (2017, April 21). Valencia, Osceola schools team up to train more teachers. *Orlando Sentinel.* Retrieved from http://www.orlandosentinel.com/features/education/school-zone/os-valencia-osceola-teacher-shortage-20170413-story.html

Schmader, T., & Johns, M. (2003). Converging evidence that stereotype threat reduces working memory capacity. *Journal of Personality and Social Psychology, 85*(3), 440-452.

Spencer, S. J., Steele, C. M., & Quinn, D. M. (1998). Stereotype threat and women's math performance. *Journal of Experimental Social Psychology, 35,* 4-28.

Steele, C. M. (1999). Thin ice: "Stereotype threat" and Black college students. *The Atlantic, 284*(2), 44-54.

Steele, C. M., & Aronson, J. (1995). Stereotype threat and the intellectual test performance of African Americans. *Journal of Personality and Social Psychology, 69*(5), 797-811.

Sutcher, L., Darling-Hammond, L., & Carver-Thomas, D. (2016). *A coming crisis in teaching? Teacher supply, demand, and shortages in the U.S.* Palo Alto, CA: Learning Policy Institute.

Thoman, D., Smith, J., Brown, E., Chase, J., & Lee, J. Y. K. (2013). Beyond performance: A motivational experiences model of stereotype threat. *Educational Psychology Review, 25*(?), 211-243.

UCF Office of Institutional Research. (2016). *UCF Florida College System consortium partners' student success feedback report: Valencia College 2015-2016.* Orlando, FL: University of Central Florida.

UCF Office of Operational Excellence and Assessment Support. (2014). *Engaging Latino students: For transfer and college completion.* Orlando, FL: University of Central Florida.

U.S. Census Bureau. (2013). *Educational attainment: 2010-2012 American community survey 3-year estimates* [Data file]. Retrieved from https://factfinder.census.gov/faces/tableservices/jsf/pages/productview.xhtml?pid=ACS_12_3YR_S1501&prodType=table

Valencia College. (2008). *Valencia Community College strategic plan 2008-13.* Retrieved from http://valenciacollege.edu/academic-affairs/institutional-effectiveness-planning/strategic-plan/documents/StrategicPlanBrochure.pdf

Valencia College Institutional Research. (2016). *Orange & Osceola County market share of previous year public high school graduates: Fall end of term* [Data file]. Retrieved from http://valenciacollege.edu/academic-affairs/institutional-effectiveness-planning/institutional-research/Reporting/Strategic-Indicators/MarketShare.cfm

Valencia College Institutional Research. (2017a). *Student characteristics* [Data file]. Retrieved from http://valenciacollege.edu/academic-affairs/institutional-effectiveness-planning/institutional-research/Reporting/Strategic-Indicators/StudentCharacteristics.cfm

Valencia College Institutional Research. (2017b). *Student progression* [Data file]. Retrieved from http://valenciacollege.edu/academic-affairs/institutional-effectiveness-planning/institutional-research/Reporting/Strategic-Indicators/StrategicIndicators.cfm

Walton, G. M., & Cohen, J. L. (2007). A question of belonging: Race, social fit, and achievement. *Journal of Personality & Social Psychology, 92*(1), 82-96.

Watts, J. (2013). Why hyperbonding occurs in the learning community classroom and what to do about it. *Learning Communities Research and Practice, 1*(3), Article 4. Retrieved from http://washingtoncenter.evergreen.edu/lcrpjournal/vol1/iss3/4

CHAPTER 7

UNDERSTANDING AND USING ASSESSMENT PRACTICES IN THE CONTEXT OF THE TRANSFER STUDENT EXPERIENCE

Kristin Moser

Assessment within higher education has continuously evolved over time (Adelman, 2009; Pace, 1979; Shavelson, 2007). Throughout this progression, assessment efforts largely focused on pockets of university students—for example, those within the general education curriculum entering an institution as first-year students. Frequently, these assessment measures involved the collection of retention rates, graduation rates, standardized test scores, and other traditional markers of student progress and achievement, which are difficult to collect for students who began their academic career at another institution. As a result, the transfer student population has been excluded entirely from these measures. As Brown and Rhodes (2016) indicate, this narrow assessment of student success and progress has made it challenging to tell the true story of the transfer student experience, as the paths that many transfer students take to four-year colleges and universities are so varied and complex. Rather than address this measurement issue, many institutions have looked upon assessment as a box to check off in the completion of mandated reports, therefore underutilizing what could be an important institutional measure of student success if collected and examined appropriately.

While transfer has often been excluded from traditional assessment models, new calls for more inclusive formulas for measuring student success have created momentum for this effort. With careful planning and data collection, these increased calls can be used as an opportunity to expand existing transfer student success programming while simultaneously providing a chance to showcase the great work happening with transfer students across the country. Thankfully, recent data collected by the American Association of Colleges and Universities (AAC&U, 2016) show this is already occurring. In a national survey of chief academic officers, higher education professionals are moving away from using standardized quantitative measures (e.g., time to degree), toward assessing cumulative learning within courses and departments across their campuses (AAC&U, 2016). What was once considered an administrative mandate has now become an effective tool in demonstrating the impact of programming on student success. This change in focus allows institutions to articulate a more complete story of student success— one that includes transfer.

Over the past several decades, enrollment managers and admissions directors have mostly focused on the traditional first-year student enrolling immediately after high school. Transfer students have always enrolled at higher education institutions; however, they have infrequently been seen as the priority in large-scale recruitment initiatives. They rarely garner as much attention from admissions counselors and other university contacts as traditional first-year students. This trend changed in the decade following the 2007 recession (Juszkiewicz, 2016), which sent many individuals into job training and technical programs at the community college level (Barr & Turner, 2013). Stimulus money propelling students to enroll at two-year institutions also encouraged transfer to four-year degree programs, thus growing transfer enrollment at baccalaureate-granting institutions across the country. When the recession ended and the economy recovered, enrollments at community colleges dropped precipitously. At the same time, states began tightening their budgets, resulting in a decrease in monetary support for higher education institutions nationally. Thus, a decrease in enrollment of transfer students was felt at a much deeper level than in years past. As the tuition collected from transfer students decreased, four-year colleges and universities began an intentional effort to recruit transfer students. The need for more institutional dollars also prompted these institutions to increase investments in programming and other efforts targeted specially at transfer students in an effort to increase their persistence.

Almost half of all students who graduated with a four-year degree in 2015-2016 had been enrolled at a two-year public institution at least once in the previous 10 years (National Student Clearinghouse, 2017). In addition, 49% obtained their degree within three years of having been enrolled at a two-year institution. However, the standard process for measuring postsecondary educational attainment at the federal level includes the first-time full-time (FTFT) freshman cohort, excluding students who start at one institution and transfer to another. Therefore, a large number of students enrolled at four-year colleges and universities across the nation go uncounted in the reporting of retention and graduation rates at higher education institutions. In a time of increasing calls for transparency and accountability, institutions are seeking better indicators of student success in an effort to accurately track all students at their institutions, regardless of institution of origin.

This chapter will review changing policy and trends related to transfer students and highlight how the careful assessment of transfer initiatives within the higher education landscape can influence transfer student success. As seen in Figure 7.1, the development of transfer programming and the assessment of its value must be deliberate, collaborative, and focused on data that include the measurement of student outcomes (Brown & Rhodes, 2016). Using this campus change process as the framework, I will discuss implications for institutions in each stage of the process. Central to this method is collaboration between divisions across campus. Student success and the collection of success measures cannot be conducted in individual silos at the institution. Instead, Brown and Rhodes (2016) stress the importance of team building across divisions, connecting administrators, faculty, and staff in this effort. This collaboration must be informed by a thorough understanding of the transfer experience at each institution, accompanied by a review of institutional policy and programming designed to address the needs of the transfer student population. Within this examination, institutions should also analyze existing data, including learning outcomes and usage patterns. Finally, for the effort to be sustainable, it is essential to connect this work with existing projects and strategic initiatives that are a priority for this institution. This will ensure the work is not superseded by other institutional priorities.

Knowledge of the Transfer Experience		
Understand the transfer pathway at your institution	Extensive review of current transfer programming	
Set Collaborative Tone Early		
Consider adopting Foundations of Excellence or CAS standards to guide practice	Cross-divisional team	Campus-wide involvement
Thorough Analysis of Existing Data and Assessments		
How does your institution define success?	Is collection systematic/ institutionalized?	How does your institution currently communicate data?
Focus on Outcomes		
Academic and cocurricular	Transfer-specific vs. university-wide outcomes	Alignment with mission and vision
Balance the Work of Existing Initiatives		
Align departments and programs doing similar work	Connect to larger, more strategic initiatives	Scaffold projects over time

Figure 7.1. Campus change process. Adapted from Brown & Rhodes (2016).

Data and the Transfer Pathway

Within federal reporting standards (e.g., National Center for Education Statistics or NCES, Integrated Postsecondary Education Data System or IPEDS), institutions use a cohort model to follow a group of students at one institution. The definitions of the cohort are extremely precise, allowing for the inclusion of students who have enrolled full time at the institution immediately after their high school graduation. While this approach provides valuable data for students and parents considering enrollment at various institutions, it does not fully show the complex nature of measuring the success of students currently enrolled in postsecondary institutions.

To counteract this discrepancy, alternative models have been developed to incorporate measures of transfer student success into overall success metrics for higher education institutions. The Student Achievement Measure (SAM, 2013) was developed to gather a more inclusive cohort of students, including those who have enrolled at more than one institution during their college career. This measure allows for an expanded definition of success, more representative of the diversity seen in student populations at institutions across the country. Therefore, while traditional measures of student success and attainment have centered on metrics related to retention and graduation of the FTFT cohort only, the SAM methodology incorporates transfer into this measure. It does so in two ways: (a) by following students from the FTFT cohort who transfer from their first institution of enrollment and (b) by adding a transfer student cohort to track completion rates (at the transfer institution or any other subsequent institutions after initial enrollment at the transfer institution).

Much of the policy related to measuring success has focused on the numbers, such as enrollment, retention, and completion rates (Rhodes, 2012). Brown and Rhodes (2016) also acknowledge the difficulties in measuring transfer student success in terms of timely graduation from a four-year institution. They argue that a shift in focus is needed to better understand the true impact of our academic and cocurricular programming on student success and student learning. The Degree Qualifications Profile (DQP), a collaborative effort of AAC&U and the Lumina Foundation (Adelman, Ewell, Gaston, & Schneider, 2011), is designed to respond to these challenges. By focusing on the student rather than the institution, the DQP allows the measure of success to translate across institutions as the student moves from the two-year college to the four-year institution. It intentionally samples a variety of knowledge and skills that all students should possess upon completion of a bachelor's degree. This profile encompasses specialized content knowledge, broad integrative knowledge, intellectual skills, applied learning, civic learning, and institution-specific measures of student learning (Adelman et al., 2011). The unique focus on the student within the DQP provides insight into learning and growth independent of standard metrics for achievement, offering institutions a framework from which to measure student development, progress, and learning attainment.

AAC&U has become a leader in assessment with the publication of its Valid Assessment of Learning in Undergraduate Education (VALUE) rubrics (Rhodes, 2009), available for institutions to use and adapt as they develop assessment plans. Rhodes (2012) indicates the VALUE rubrics arose from the need to more clearly define the meaning of the undergraduate degree.

> One of the most surprising findings to emerge from the employer surveys was that the college transcript, with its list of titles, grades, and credits, was not very useful in helping employers select graduates who were likely to be successful in their companies. The transcript did not adequately represent what an individual student could actually do with her/his learning. Therefore, other measures and indicators were needed. (p. 37)

Not only were employers asking for a more tangible form of evidence related to college student outcomes; accreditors also began to demand more substance in institutional assessment of student learning, thus hastening the collection of data within this context at institutions across the country.

In 2015, the Liberal Education and America's Promise (LEAP) Challenge worked to engage not only higher education but also the public in the promotion and adoption of standards related to assessment, high-impact educational practices, and the establishment of measurable and meaningful learning outcomes (AAC&U, 2015a). This initiative expanded upon the AAC&U VALUE rubrics (Rhodes, 2009) by emphasizing the role of *signature work*, defined as educational experiences that provide students with problem-solving opportunities to develop the skills necessary to succeed after graduation. The use of the signature work model allows students to explore issues from multiple viewpoints and perspectives, often outside of any one discipline (AAC&U, 2015b). Using the LEAP model and the signature work framework, institutions can demonstrate the impact of the delivered educational experience on all students, regardless of institution of origin. The framework is principally relevant when measuring transfer student success as it focuses on essential learning outcomes that all students must attain, regardless of where they began their postsecondary career. This focus on signature work requires students to use cumulative learning experiences to solve a problem or question over the course of one semester, at minimum. The signature work model is particularly attractive to external stakeholders who are demanding more evidence and assurance that the graduates they hire have the knowledge and skills needed to succeed in the workplace.

An additional technique to measure success and improve practice within transfer student populations is adoption of the Council for the Advancement of Standards in Higher Education (CAS) guidelines. First published almost 40 years ago (CAS, 2015), these guidelines continue to provide a framework for institutions to assess the programming and services offered to students outside of the classroom. The guidelines outline 45 professional standards through which institutions measure impact and effectiveness of programming. From a transfer perspective, the CAS standards allow an institution to determine whether it has a transfer-receptive culture (Marling, 2013), which is critical in the success of transfer students at four-year institutions. This culture is highlighted by pre-transfer efforts, including an intentional focus on access for transfer students at four-year institutions as well as formal outreach and transfer programming (Marling, 2013). Post-transfer initiatives that provide a culture conducive to transfer success include institutional understanding of the unique experience and needs of the transfer population, broad institutional support of these students (both academic and financial), and systematic evaluation of programming designed to meet their needs (Marling, 2013). The CAS standards provide tools to assess a broad spectrum of services, ranging from orientation to career services to campus activities. Through a self-assessment process, institutions gauge the impact of student services and student development opportunities within student affairs divisions. This allows institutions to take a holistic approach to the assessment of services, using the entire student-lived experience, both inside and outside the classroom.

While a comprehensive institutional assessment can help gauge systematic efforts related to transfer, it is also important to include the examination of transfer students as individuals. Various psychosocial factors have an impact on transfer student adjustment and play a central role in the evaluation of institutional transfer programming. Laanan (2004) and Moser (2013) detail the development and refinement of a construct called *transfer student capital* (i.e., academic advising experiences, perceptions of the transfer process, experiences with community college faculty, learning and study skills, financial literacy, and motivation and self-efficacy). Within the theory of transfer student capital, the greater amount of this capital a student acquires while at the community college, the greater their success at the four-year transfer destination (Laanan, Starobin, & Eggleston, 2011; Moser, 2013). Students with higher levels of transfer student capital performed better academically, were better able to cope with their problems at their four-year transfer destination, and were more satisfied with academics and advising than students with lower levels of this capital (Moser, 2013). These findings illustrate the importance of moving beyond traditional success measures (e.g., retention, graduation rates) to a more robust evaluation of the student experience.

Collaboration as a Key to Development and Implementation

Cross-divisional collaboration is a critical component of any successful assessment effort within an institution. We often reference silos on college campuses, with individual faculty, staff, and departments working independently to advance their students. For true and meaningful assessment of transfer students to occur, the academic side of the institution must work in tandem with student affairs and other student development offices. A model for this type of effort can be seen in the Foundations of Excellence (FOE) process developed by the Gardner Institute for Excellence in Undergraduate Education (2017). The FOE model requires institutions to engage in an intensive self-study, working with colleagues in other divisions to create a list of actions needed to spur momentum in first-year or transfer efforts. At the University of Northern Iowa (UNI), this process led to a fundamental change in how divisions worked together in subsequent efforts. The emphasis on partnerships between academic and student affairs was so successful at UNI that it continues to be adopted for new committees or councils at the institution. The collaborative nature of FOE has resulted in streamlined data collection efforts and assessment efforts at UNI, with the campus routinely sharing data on various programs for transfer students, among other populations.

For an institution engaged in an intensive self-study such as that promoted within the FOE experience or from the CAS guidelines, an inventory of current practices provides valued insight on where to focus institutional efforts related to transfer programming. An examination of all aspects of the institution is necessary to prioritize efforts for transfer students. For example, admissions processes, orientation/new student registration, financial aid and scholarships available to transfers, academic articulation and course credits accepted, housing, and engagement opportunities should, at the very least, be documented and hopefully modified to better serve the institutional mission. The ultimate goal of these actions is to impact transfer students and increase their success at the institution and beyond.

Another area of focus related to collaboration occurs between community colleges and four-year institutions. This is often a relationship overlooked in the assessment of transfer initiatives. If an institution is truly interested in the success of its students, deliberate relationships must exist between institutions. Brown and Rhodes (2016) detail the development of the Degree Qualifications Profile and the extensive collaboration that took place in institutions across the country during this effort. In one example, James Madison University and Blue Ridge Community College partnered in a variety of ways, including the use of common assessment instruments and cross-institutional data sharing (Brown & Rhodes, 2016). In Indiana, a state legislative mandate resulted in a common general education transfer core. Individuals from multiple institutions across the state, with representation from both two-year and four-year institutions, used this mandate as an opportunity to come together to develop common core learning outcomes that would be measured and assessed at all institutions regardless of type (Brown & Rhodes, 2016). Collaboration and campus-wide involvement played a key role in the success of these efforts. Such inter-institutional communication will enhance the student experience at both institution types and ultimately result in positive student learning, growth, and development.

Institutional Analysis of Transfer Data

Assessment can directly impact classroom teaching and student learning, but the evaluation of transfer programming often requires an additional set of statistical analyses to determine its impact. This evaluation can be complicated by small numbers of transfers and the difficulty of creating and tracking cohorts; this requires individuals within the institution to work collaboratively to collect data from a variety of programs and other assessment sources available on campus. Individuals can do much of this work using information collected internally; however, some external data sources, such as IPEDS, should also be considered, as these reports are required by the federal (and sometimes state) government and are readily available at any institution receiving federal funding. Using a combination of qualitative and quantitative components from a variety of sources will give a robust data set that can be used to determine the effectiveness of transfer student programming at the institution. Data points that should be collected include, but are not limited to, academic performance (e.g., course grade, semester GPA); retention; student engagement measures (e.g., National Survey of Student Engagement [NSSE]); pre- and post-tests of student attitudes, satisfaction, and self-perceived gains; degree attainment; and direct measures of student learning.

Given the various reporting requirements for higher education, most institutions should at minimum have some sort of baseline for measuring progress within their transfer efforts. An institution might not have the infrastructure to engage in full-fledged assessment and evaluation of these efforts; while this may point to broader issues from an institutional priority perspective, it can still be addressed by using a variety of existing federally required reports. One such report is the Outcomes Measures component of the IPEDS annual reporting cycle. First implemented in 2015, the Outcomes Measures section was designed to address the growing diversity of students in postsecondary education, particularly among students transferring to other institutions who historically have been excluded from any real reporting or accountability measures. In an effort to broaden student outcome measures reported at the federal level, IPEDS added several new cohort reporting requirements in addition to the traditional FTFT cohort. The new cohorts included first-time, part-time students and non-first-time, full- and part-time students (i.e., transfer students). An institution wanting to gauge the success of its incoming transfer students can use this report to gain a better understanding of how those students are progressing. While not a direct one-to-one comparison with the traditional first-time-in-college cohort, this new measure provides a great baseline from which institutions can demonstrate growth and success of transfer student populations. It also allows an institution to benchmark progress and success rates with peer institutions across the country, providing important context in the effort to understand transfer dynamics at the institution.

While examining the existing data is useful, it only tells part of the story related to the transfer experience. The information collected from existing data sources on campus can be used to complement the evidence being gathered to examine the impact of various interventions and programming efforts at the institution. Data on transfer programming can be collected in a variety of ways including, but not limited to, student opinion surveys, pre- and post-tests related to aptitude in a specific discipline or around certain core skills, faculty feedback surveys, and the measurement of student learning outcomes. Working closely with the institutional research office at an institution will yield a wealth of information related to student background, college preparation, and socioeconomic status. A knowledgeable evaluator will combine data obtained from multiple sources to create a large data set encompassing a wide variety of outputs and measures.

The next logical progression after compiling these data is to create a series of comparison groups for established transfer cohorts at the institution. While it may be tempting to compare new transfer students (e.g., students entering the institution with an associate degree) to native juniors at the institution when measuring persistence rates, it is important to note the differences between these groups of students. For example, a student still enrolled at the institution as a junior has already demonstrated the ability to succeed at the school, evidenced by their retention into their junior year. This also illustrates the need to consider measures other than traditional markers of success, such as retention rate.

Creating a unique comparison group using institutional data and a matched sample design is one way to avoid this problem. For example, if an institution needs to assess the impact of a new series of supportive seminars linked to a course in which transfer students typically struggle, an evaluator may initially start by examining the grades of students who took the seminar and comparing them with grades of those in the same course who did not take the seminar. Initial results may not yield positive findings related to the intervention (i.e., the supportive seminar). However, it is possible that only those students struggling the most academically attended the seminar. Therefore, the evaluator may be comparing the least academically prepared students with the students who would be expected to have the highest achievement in the course. Instead of this approach, the evaluator should use the institutional data collected previously to link the students on various characteristics known to influence academic performance (e.g., transfer GPA) to create a matched sample. Using a matched sample essentially allows the researcher to create a situation that somewhat mimics an experimental design. The matched sample will then be used as a comparison group for the students who attended the seminar to those who did not but who are matched academically or otherwise.

Academic success in higher education is linked to several student background characteristics and precollege experiences (Kuh, Kinzie, Buckley, Bridges, & Hayek, 2006). Often, subjects are matched on factors known to impact student success at the institution. Some of these factors are considered more demographic in nature (e.g., academic preparation, race/ethnicity, first-generation status) while others are considered more behavioral or social (e.g., student engagement and involvement on campus). All must be considered when evaluating the success of transfer students; therefore, it is important to include these factors when matching the samples for this type of analysis. Perhaps there exists a sample of students who participated in a targeted transfer program, one designed to connect new transfer students with other transfers in a community-building effort. If the goal is to test the impact or the effectiveness of the program, it is necessary to compare the students who participated with a group of similar students who did not, matching on characteristics like those described above.

Focus on Outcomes: A Case Study at the University of Northern Iowa

According to Blaylock and Bresciani (2011), successful transfer programming requires institutional commitment to the mission of transfer success. Through the transfer mission comes an alignment of resources with transfer success outcomes. Integrated assessment and measurement of program effectiveness will result in further support of transfer initiatives and a strategic impact on decision makers at the institution. UNI recently adopted a new strategic enrollment master plan. Within this plan are specific indicators targeting transfer students, ranging from recruitment to retention and completion rates for transfer students. The goal is to attract transfers, mainly from community colleges, while improving their success rates to match those of native students. Loan indebtedness is also considered, ensuring that transfer students are not borrowing more than is needed. These goals are closely aligned with the hallmarks of a transfer-receptive culture (Marling, 2013) and resulted in an institution-wide call to action to improve the transfer student experience.

These enrollment targets led to the development of various programs designed to address the unique experiences and needs of transfer students. From the very beginning, the programs were linked to various theories in student success literature and developed using the framework highlighted within the theories. The work of Tinto (1997, 2000) was central to development of the new programming at UNI. Astin's Input-Environment-Outcomes (I-E-O) model (Astin, 1993) served as a framework to analyze these efforts, using the inputs (i.e., the demographic characteristics of the student at the time of entry to the institution) together with the institutional program type and frequency of participation (environment), to determine student success (outcome). The impact of the initiative(s) on student success was then evaluated. As various student outcomes were measured (e.g., retention into the next year, semester GPA, graduation rate), the institution was able to infer that participation in the program resulted in increases for the intervention group, given that the samples were matched on the remaining factors known to impact student success in college.

It was necessary to adapt the theoretical frameworks from Astin (1993) and Tinto (1997) during the development process for the programming at UNI, incorporating additional factors specific to transfer student success, as both of their models tend to apply to traditional college students who begin their education as new first-year students at the institution. Criticisms of the adaptability of Tinto's theory to the transfer student population (Braxton, Hirschy, & McClendon, 2004) call for the adaptation of the model to include various factors that are often unique to transfer students. In the Braxton et al. model (2004), social integration is central to student success and is characterized by a culture for concern for student growth and development that is central to institutional programming. Student perception of membership in the campus social environment, with an emphasis on relationships with peers, is critical to successful integration in the campus community (Braxton et al., 2004). According to Braxton et al. (2014), social integration is a strong mediator among student entry characteristics (e.g., high school achievement, family socioeconomic status), institutional inputs (e.g., institutional commitment), and student persistence. Social integration is influenced by four key factors related to student success: (a) ability to pay, (b) institutional commitment to student welfare, (c) institutional integrity, and (d) psychosocial engagement (Braxton et al., 2014). Cabrera, Stampen, and Hansen (1990) found that inability to pay acts as a significant barrier to student participation in the social communities on college campuses. Braxton et al. (2014) found that the degree of satisfaction students had regarding the cost of attendance strongly influenced their social integration on the new campus. With the knowledge that transfer students tend to be more diverse financially, this factor is a critical component in their success at the four-year institution.

Institutional commitment to student welfare also has a profound effect on social integration of the student. Again, this references the culture of care and concern that permeates the institution and a student's perception that they are valued and respected as individuals and contributors to the campus community (Braxton et al., 2004). Transfer students arrive at their new institution after having close connections with faculty and staff at their community college (Moser, 2013). If they do not feel valued and respected as they join the university community, their social integration is negatively impacted. Related to this is the impact of institutional integrity on social integration, more specifically whether students perceive that institutional representatives (i.e., faculty and staff) are congruent with the mission and goals of the institution (Braxton et al., 2014). Finally, the psychosocial engagement of the student is critical to their integration socially. A student must invest in their social experience, participating with peers and engaging in extracurricular activities for social integration to occur (Braxton et al., 2004).

Balance the Work of Existing Initiatives

At UNI, one such initiative aimed at improving student success and social integration is the Peer Mentoring Program, designed to reach students through curricular programming within the first year. Developing this programming involved focused collaboration from academic and student affairs units on campus. Using a classroom as community model originally inspired by the work of Tinto (1997, 2000) and Braxton et al. (2004, 2014), peers were placed into certain sections of the general education curriculum to serve as mentors to their fellow students. As Tinto (1997) noted,

> for students who commute to college, especially those who have multiple obligations outside the college, the classroom may be the only place where students and faculty meet. ... For these students in particular, ... If academic and social involvement or integration is to occur, it must occur in the classroom. (p. 599)

The program was designed with this in mind, as reflected in UNI's First-Year Philosophy Statement, which reads as follows:

> A positive first-year experience is the cornerstone of students' success in college, and by extension, their careers and lives. The University of Northern Iowa recognizes the importance and value of this positive first-year experience for students, and the need for the university to facilitate students' effective transition to the University by providing a variety of experiences, opportunities, and foundational skills to help them become successful students (Chatham-Carpenter, Heistad, Licari, Moser, & Woods, 2014, p. 2).

This statement directly addresses the commitment of the institution to positive student experiences and illustrates how faculty and staff will be working to achieve these goals within their daily work. The institution was intentional in the design of a rigorous academic classroom experience, coupling that with the necessary resources (e.g., transition, academic, financial, and psychosocial support) for student success (Chatham-Carpenter et al., 2014).

The goal of embedding additional resources within the academic course allowed for the work of the peer mentor, who engaged with faculty to deliver content specific to student needs in the course as well as other transition issues (Chatham-Carpenter et al., 2014). The peer mentor works to build community within the classroom and mentor first-year students. Five specific outcomes are related to the peer mentor program at UNI, as well as a stipulation that the peer mentor completes 10 hours per week working with students in their assigned course, which they have already successfully completed in their first year at the institution (Chatham-Carpenter et al., 2014). The five outcomes for peer mentors include (a) holding regular office hours, (b) participating in a peer mentoring seminar, (c) attending every class session of the assigned course, (d) assisting the faculty member in the classroom, and (e) mentoring individual students in and outside the classroom (Chatham-Carpenter et al., 2014).

Careful planning began prior to the launch of this initiative, with assessment opportunities built in at the ground level. The team was committed to the collection and dissemination of data related to programming efforts early on in the process. The gathering of data and feedback from all levels of this initiative (including student participants, peer mentors, and the faculty teaching these courses) was critical in the establishment and development of future programming. Through careful collection of these data during the pilot year and in subsequent years, analysis of the true impact on student success, and dissemination of these data to decision makers at the institution, the developers of this programming received funding to expand the program. The peer mentoring program grew from eight sections of general education classes serving 381 distinct students, to 15 sections of courses serving 662 distinct students (Chatham-Carpenter et al., 2014).

Given the linkage to the academic classroom, data on program effectiveness were intentionally and strategically disseminated to faculty groups on campus (Heistad, Moser, & Woods, 2016). Once the connection between successful student transition/adjustment and academic performance was made, faculty across campus began to understand how vital the first-year transition period was (Chatham-Carpenter et al., 2014). More specifically, during the pilot year of the program and in subsequent years, information was collected at a variety of points throughout the semester and combined into a large data set to examine the impact of this programming on student success (Chatham-Carpenter et al., 2014). Various institutional data points were also examined (e.g., ACT score, race/ethnicity, university GPA) to determine the impact on student grades, retention, and graduation. Students in these courses were retained at a rate of 6-8% higher than students who did not take a first-year course with an embedded peer mentor. These students also had significantly higher perceived communication skills compared with other first-year students ($p < .05$). Therefore, the impact of peer mentoring could be seen in student retention and graduation, an important metric at the university. As these data were shared with campus constituents and administrators at the institution, funding was expanded to add additional peer mentor-supported sections, including additional transfer-only courses within the general education curriculum.

As the UNI case study illustrates, mechanisms for transfer student success can be identified and eventually expanded when institutional commitment to enhancing the transfer experience is solidified, specific programming is established, and data collection and assessment are conducted in a systematic and intentional manner. At UNI, statistical evidence indicated that students in the peer mentor-enhanced sections of the general education curriculum were retained more often than comparable students not taking courses with a peer mentor (Chatham-Carpenter et al., 2014), resulting in expansion of the programming to include more transfer students. More importantly, this programming positively impacted a greater number of transfer students, resulting in increased success and achievement for these students.

Conclusions and Recommendations

There is an increased focus on measuring success of transfer students at the national level. This focus, while well intentioned, requires additional vetting and consensus before higher education institutions can move to a national model that is agreed upon by everyone. Meanwhile, there is a need to continue to advocate for programming and support initiatives for transfer students on our own campuses. This means that institutions must continue to assess their strategic focus, collect data on the effectiveness of programs, and be the voice of transfer students at the institutional level.

Data that explain the impact of transfer programming on student transition and success can be used to advocate for this programming in times of decreasing state budgets and other competing priorities in higher education. A wide variety of frameworks and data analysis options are available to assist in the evaluation and assessment of transfer programs. Collecting program data in diverse formats and from a variety of sources (e.g., students, faculty) helps demonstrate the impact of programming efforts at multiple levels within the organization, provides key decision makers with the information needed to move in strategic directions, and allows the institution to tell its story to both internal and external stakeholders.

Collaboration is key to the sustainability of any programming. As previously mentioned, the FOE experience created synergies with areas and individuals on campus where there had been none previously. The collaborative nature of the work on campus became part of the culture after undergoing the FOE process. At UNI, a cooperative relationship between faculty and various offices on campus (i.e., Student Success and Retention, Institutional Research and Effectiveness, Undergraduate Studies, and Academic Advising) resulted in successful collaboration to promote the expansion of peer mentor programming, largely buoyed by the analysis of the impact of these programs.

Sustainability is a key aspect when evaluating program data and the possibility of long-term success. Data collected should be shared widely on campus with faculty and student success professionals who are passionate about the work they do with transfers, as well as with institutional administrators responsible for continued funding of these efforts. Further, the measurement of student success, a focus on sustainability, and deliberate faculty development related to the transfer experience are central to the institutionalization and enhancement of transfer support programs.

References

Adelman, C. (2009). *The Bologna Process for U.S. eyes: Relearning higher education in the age of convergence.* Washington, DC: Institute for Higher Education Policy.

Adelman, C., Ewell, P., Gaston, P., & Schneider, C. G. (2011). *The Degree Qualifications Profile. Defining degrees: A new direction for American higher education to be tested and developed in partnership with faculty, students, leaders and stakeholders.* Indianapolis, IN: Lumina Foundation for Education.

Association of American Colleges & Universities (AAC&U). (2015a). *The LEAP challenge: Education for a world of unscripted problems.* Retrieved from https://www.aacu.org/sites/default/files/files/LEAP/IntroToLEAP2015.pdf

Association of American Colleges & Universities (AAC&U). (2015b). *LEAP signature work.* Retrieved from https://www.aacu.org/sites/default/files/files/LEAP/LEAPChallengeSignatureWork.pdf

Association of American Colleges & Universities (AAC&U). (2016). *Trends in learning outcomes assessment: Key findings from a survey among administrators at AAC&U member institutions.* Retrieved from https://www.aacu.org/publications-research/publications/trends-learning-outcomes-assessment-key-findings-survey-among

Astin, A. W. (1993). *What matters in college?* San Francisco, CA: Jossey-Bass.

Barr, A., & Turner, S. E. (2013). Expanding enrollments and contracting state budgets: The effect of the great recession on higher education. *The Annals of the American Academy of Political and Social Science, 650,* 168-193.

Blaylock, R. S., & Bresciani, M. J. (2011). Exploring the success of transfer programs for community college students. *Research & Practice in Assessment, 6,* 43-61.

Braxton, J. M., Doyle, W. R., Hartley, H. V., Hirschy, A. S., Jones, W. A., & McLendon, M. K. (2014). *Rethinking college student retention.* San Francisco, CA: Wiley & Sons.

Braxton, J. M., Hirschy, A. S., & McClendon, S. A. (2004). *Understanding and reducing college student departure.* San Francisco, CA: Jossey-Bass.

Brown, G. R., & Rhodes, T. L. (2016). *Assessment practices for advancing transfer student success: Collaborating for educational change.* Washington, DC: Association of American Colleges and Universities.

Cabrera, A. F., Stampen, J. O., & Hansen, W. L. (1990). Exploring the effects of ability to pay on persistence in college. *The Review of Higher Education, 13*(3), 303-336.

Chatham-Carpenter, A., Heistad, D., Licari, M., Moser, K., & Woods, K. (2014). Creating classroom communities: Faculty & peer mentor collaboration in first-year only classes. In S. Whalen (Ed.), *Proceedings of the 10th National Symposium on Student Retention,* Louisville, KY (pp. 73-84). Norman, OK: The University of Oklahoma.

Council for the Advancement of Standards in Higher Education (2015). *CAS professional standards for higher education* (9th ed.). Washington, DC: Author.

Gardner Institute for Excellence in Undergraduate Education. (2017). *Foundations of excellence.* Retrieved from http://www.jngi.org/foundations-of-excellence

Heistad, D., Moser, K., & Woods, K. (2016). Meeting students where they are: A practical guide to embedding retention initiatives in the general education classroom. In G. McLaughlin, R. Howard, J. McLaughlin, & W. E. Knight (Eds.), *Building bridges for student success: A sourcebook for colleges and universities* (pp. 462-476). Norman, OK: Consortium for Student Retention Data Exchange.

Juszkiewicz, J. (2016). *Trends in community college enrollment and completion data.* Washington, DC: American Association of Community Colleges.

Kuh, G. D., Kinzie, J., Buckley, J. A., Bridges, B. K., & Hayek, J. C. (2006). *Spearheading a dialog on student success* [Commissioned report for the National Symposium on Postsecondary Student Success]. Washington, DC: National Postsecondary Education Cooperative.

Laanan, F. S. (2004). Studying transfer students: Part 1: Instrument design and implications. *Community College Journal of Research and Practice, 28,* 331-351. doi:10.1080/10668920490424050

Laanan, F. S., Starobin, S. S., & Eggleston, L. E. (2011). Adjustment of community college students at a four-year university: Role and relevance of transfer student capital for student retention. *Journal of College Student Retention, 12*(2), 175-209. doi:10.2190/CS.12.2.d

Marling, J. L. (Ed.) (2013). *Collegiate transfer: Navigating the new normal* (New Directions for Higher Education, No. 162). San Francisco, CA: Jossey-Bass.

Moser, K. M. (2013). Exploring the impact of transfer capital on community college transfer students. *Journal of The First-Year Experience & Students in Transition, 25*(2), 53-75.

National Student Clearinghouse. (2017). *Snapshot report: Contribution of two-year institutions to four-year completions.* Retrieved from https://nscblog.org/2017/03/49-percent-of-2015-16-bachelors-degree-earners-previously-enrolled-at-two-year-public-institutions/

Pace, C. R. (1979). *Measuring outcomes of college. Fifty years of findings and recommendations for the future.* San Francisco, CA: Jossey-Bass.

Rhodes, T. (2009). *Assessing outcomes and improving achievement: Tips and tools for using the rubrics.* Washington, DC: Association of American Colleges and Universities.

Rhodes, T. (2012). Show me the learning: Value, accreditation, and the quality of the degree: Higher education now has both tools and frameworks for organizing and connecting teaching and learning in a meaningful way. *Planning for Higher Education, 40*(3), 26-42.

Shavelson, R. J. (2007). *A brief history of student learning assessment: How we got where we are and a proposal for where to go next.* Washington, DC: Association of American Colleges and Universities.

Student Achievement Measure (SAM). (2013). *About.* Retrieved from http://www.studentachievementmeasure.org/about

Tinto, V. (1997). Classrooms as communities: Exploring the educational character of student persistence. *Journal of Higher Education, 68*(6), 599-623.

Tinto, V. (2000). Linking learning and leaving: Exploring the role of the college classroom in student departure. In J. M. Braxton (Ed.), *Reworking the student departure puzzle* (pp. 81-94). Nashville, TN: Vanderbilt University Press.

CHAPTER **8**

CONCLUSION **▌**

Mark Allen Poisel and Sonya Joseph

As the focus on and demand for accountability in postsecondary education increase, there is greater urgency to address the challenges and opportunities faced by transfer students and the institutions that serve them. Flat or declining numbers of high school graduates (Anderson, 2016), increased credentialing needs for employment, and the socioeconomic impact of degree completion on individuals will shape how higher education entities view the importance of transfer students for the foreseeable future. As described in Chapter 1, transfer students frequently take a nonlinear approach to postsecondary learning that can impede degree completion. By offering students clearly marked pathways to degree completion and career preparation, institutions can minimize their likelihood of not graduating.

The authors of this book describe institutional and statewide progress on initiatives designed to ensure the success of transfer students in the face of ongoing challenges. Despite continued efforts to improve the college transitions of this growing population of students, transfer pathways remain unclear for some. Work is still needed on campuses without significant or well-defined partnerships, and questions persist about the most effective ways to ensure transfer success.

Here, we reflect on three themes emerging from the book: (a) recognition of emerging patterns and pathways of transfer mobility, (b) the need for increased intentionality in institutional attention to and support for transfers, and (c) a renewed call for specially designed programs and enhanced supports for transfer students. Throughout, the authors highlight the progress made on these three fronts since the publication of *Transfer Students in Higher Education* (Poisel & Joseph, 2011). At the same time, they suggest areas in our approach to transfer students where significant work remains.

Emerging Patterns of Transfer Mobility

The pattern of direct transfer from one institution to another (i.e., community college to four-year college or university) still exists; however, more complex patterns have emerged. In part, these patterns represent an increase in mobility related to family, finances, and work, among other factors. Students may not transfer to an institution for degree completion, instead staying only long enough to complete a course or two before moving to another school. Though increased mobility has implications for institutional completion rates—a perceived indicator of educational quality—colleges and universities must dedicate resources to supporting students while they are enrolled and helping them successfully transition to their next step, whatever that may be.

Institutions may also need to reconsider how they define transfer. Students and parents take advantage of the cost-saving benefits of Advanced Placement, International Baccalaureate, and dual enrollment programs, with recent high school graduates routinely entering college with one or more semester's worth of credits earned. Such programs increase access to college credit but present a number of challenges for institutions. Among these are determining the academic rigor of college credits earned in high school; managing the intellectual, emotional, and social development of students entering college at a younger age; and supporting recent high school graduates transferring into junior-level courses. Students are being encouraged to make decisions on careers and majors much earlier, often without access to college academic advisors. They may also find themselves exhausting financial aid eligibility before they complete their degrees, if they enter with too many credits. As we think about these new challenges, more research is needed to determine the success of these students, their impact on the meaning of transfer for the institution, and ultimately the practices that help develop the transfer experience.

Intentional Focus on Transfer

A key first step in creating an intentional focus on transfer students is building an institution-specific transfer profile. Institutional data hold the key to defining the unique transfer population on a given campus. Are they community college transfers, lateral transfers from similar institutions, stop-outs returning to college, accelerated high school students, reverse transfers, military-connected students, online students, or some combination of these groups? What can institutional data tell us about the success of transfer students? How do their academic performance, progress to degree, and graduation rates compare with those who started as first-year students at the institution? How does earning credits from multiple institutions impact degree completion? Are targeted interventions having a positive impact on graduation rates—and for which students? By understanding institutional data on enrolled transfer students, practitioners build the case for greater support to help improve retention, progression, and graduation.

Institutional assessment efforts can help identify specific needs among transfer students, which in turn should drive the development and deployment of transfer support services and the removal of potential barriers to access and success. Historically, community colleges and four-year institutions have focused on creating 2 + 2 agreements. However, more consideration will be needed for 2 + 2 + 2 pathways for students who connect their accelerated high school credits to a degree path at the two-year college and into the university. Such a reframing of articulation and pathways will require institutions to deploy new advising models and orientation programs, for example. Institutions can also embrace new programming initiatives and service models, enhance support for students at all levels of academic preparedness, and adapt proven strategies for success. Finally, institutions should ensure that transfer students have access to cohort-based learning, linked courses, service-learning, undergraduate research, and other high-impact educational practices linked to gains in learning, development, and college success, especially among underserved student populations (Finley & McNair, 2013; Kuh, 2008).

Ongoing assessment efforts are also needed to ensure programs are meeting desired outcomes, the most important being student success. Program assessment efforts also help institutions address questions related to accountability, affordability, and access. They provide support for program expansion and highlight the evolving needs of this dynamic population. Finally, such assessment efforts demonstrate the need for and effectiveness of state- and institution-level partnerships around transfer success.

Assessment and data analysis can drive the strategic planning for all programs at the college or university, especially those focused on building pathways for successful transfer. With increased mobility and access, more students bring credits from such varied sources as pre-collegiate programs, the workforce experience, and the military in addition to credits earned in more traditional postsecondary programs. To respond to the wide range of prior learning and academic credit students carry with them, institutions will need to review their curriculum requirements, especially within general education; update their processes for awarding credit; and possibly change institutional strategies for supporting new students beyond what is normally provided to first-time entering students.

Enhanced Institutional Support

An intentional focus on transfer will lead to the development or refinement of specialized support programs and services, but institutional support for transfer is broader than a suite of initiatives. In this section, we explore two key areas of institutional support for transfer students—orientation and academic advising—and move beyond those to discuss larger organizing structures for supporting transfer success.

Create Specialized Orientation Initiatives

Orientations designed specifically for transfer students are essential to their success. Such programs remove barriers in the transfer process, help students manage some of the common challenges related to transfer, and connect students to the institutional resources needed to reach the appropriate pathway from the beginning. Writing in Chapter 4, Stephanie Foote urged practitioners to understand their student populations better in order to build orientations that meet the needs of various subpopulations of transfers. These include veterans and first-generation students, who might require specialized content (e.g., veteran certification or international student assimilation) or different modalities (e.g., evening, online, hybrid) to make a successful transition to a new campus. Orientation programs should also include a variety of functional areas at the college to help transfer students feel a part of the larger community.

An all-encompassing orientation program not only integrates the student into the college or university but also allows for direct communication to transfer students, as we learned for the programs at the University of Iowa and University at Albany (UAlbany) in Chapter 4. Members of the UAlbany orientation committee met with campus stakeholders and students to redesign the school's orientation program to focus on student transition, academic advising, and orientation to campus. UAlbany offers new-student orientation for transfer in two parts: (a) a one-day summer session focused on advising and course registration and (b) a one-day session immediately before classes start to focus on transition issues.

Retool Academic Advising

The philosophical underpinnings of advising—connecting with an advisor, understanding academic requirements, identifying resources, creating an educational plan, and tracking progress—define good practice regardless of the student served. That said, new transfer advising models that build upon these fundamentals are needed to serve an increasingly mobile group of students. The advising timeline needs to shift to earlier in the process to ensure students enroll in courses associated with their academic path, meet current institutional requirements, and do not repeat courses already taken at a different institution. The initial conversation changes to deepen the understanding of students' paths to this point and to make sure they understand the new institution's policies, academic requirements, and resources. In addition, special attention should be paid to transfer credit evaluation to ensure students enroll in the appropriate courses. Advisor training also should expand to include a better understanding of creating guided pathways for student success.

Define Clear Pathways

Given the highly mobile nature of today's transfer students, institutional efforts must go beyond reviewing policies and processes, adapting current support structures, and designing a boutique program for transfer students. They must also focus on creating clear pathways that lead to successful degree completion, regardless of where students began their college experience and of the number of stops in between. Thinking and operating outside the framework of traditional student cohorts and transfer student models, institutions can build pathways for students who may not historically have had access to higher education. For example, in Chapter 6, Kathleen Plinske describes El Camino, a program designed to provide a bridge for underserved students from Valencia College to the University of Central Florida.

Identify New Partnership Models

Institutional partnerships have been the foundation of transfer student success efforts for many years. Strong examples of these inter-institutional partnerships in Arizona and Florida are featured in this book. Whether they include efforts to build strong, community-based programs, increase collaboration among institutions to improve transfer pathways, or find ways to award degrees through the reverse transfer of credit, partnerships continue to play a critical role in helping transfer students complete college. Statewide partnerships, such as those in Tennessee, represent the next wave and may significantly impact transfer student success. These partnerships come with great effort, communication, and work; however, the benefits to transfer students include additional programs specifically designed for them and, more importantly, increased access and higher success rates. Through partnerships, transfer students experience guided pathways that support their movement from one institution to another while helping them maintain momentum for degree completion. State-level partnerships also impact policy that can benefit all students and help institutions better serve their student population.

Where We Go from Here

A focus on transfer students means more than recruiting and admitting them to increase headcount. Institutions must determine the role that transfer students play in goals related to access, enrollment, completion, and service to the communities where they are based. Thus, admitting transfer students and helping them achieve their educational goals are important ways to achieve institutional mandates for accessibility and accountability. Yet, the definition of transfer student is evolving, and we need to be mindful as new subpopulations of such students emerge. Drawing on the preceding discussion, we offer five strategies to rethink the importance of transfer and to prioritize the success of transfer students. These include

- ensuring that the various types of transfer and the associated academic pathways inform institutional strategic planning efforts;

- documenting student success and telling the story of transfer students on college and university campuses through well-designed data analysis;

- creating and implementing meaningful partnerships on campus, in the community, and at the state level to focus on access and student mobility;

- building programmatic initiatives to support the various and changing needs of transfer students, before and after transfer, to identify pathways for transfer students and increase their completion rate; and

- expanding the definitions of orientation and advising to ensure that a single one-size-fits-all program is not used for the transfer population.

Using institutional data to continually refine our local definition of transfer and assess progress toward desired outcomes ensures that transfer success is an intentional part of strategic planning efforts. Such efforts also ensure that institutions find the best fit for their campus and local communities.

We have not yet solved the transfer problem, but we should understand the responsibility to keep transfer students on the radar and recognize them as significant populations on campuses. The chapter authors provide information grounded in research and practice that educators can use to begin or reframe institutional conversations about transfer. It is our hope that we continue to explore the questions of how access and success become realities for all students who seek postsecondary credentials, especially those whose journeys take them through multiple educational environments.

References

Anderson, N. (2016, December 6). Supply of U.S. high school graduates is stagnating, posing challenge for colleges. *The Washington Post*. Retrieved from http://washingtonpost.com

Finley, A., & McNair, T. (2013). *Assessing underserved students' engagement in high-impact practices*. Washington, DC: Association of American Colleges & Universities.

Kuh, G. D. (2008). *High-impact educational practices: What are they, who has access to them, and why they matter*. Washington, DC: Association of American Colleges & Universities.

Poisel, M. A., & Joseph, S. (Eds.). (2011). *Transfer students in higher education: Building foundations for policies, programs, and services that foster student success* (Monograph No. 54). Columbia, SC: University of South Carolina, National Resource Center for The First-Year Experience and Students in Transition.

INDEX ▌

NOTE: Page numbers with italicized *f* or *t* indicate figures or tables respectively.

ABOUT THE CONTRIBUTORS ▌

Nancy Dietrich is the project director for statewide academic initiatives for the University of Tennessee System. In this role, she champions planning and implementation of policies and processes for transfer students, including Tennessee Reverse Transfer and Tennessee Reconnect programs. Preceding her administrative role with the University of Tennessee System, Dietrich served 12 years as an elementary teacher in the St. Charles, Missouri, City School District. She holds a BS in elementary education from Murray State University, an MA in education from Lindenwood University, and an EdD in higher education leadership from Maryville University.

Stephanie M. Foote is the assistant vice president for teaching, learning, and evidence-based practices at the Gardner Institute for Excellence in Undergraduate Education. Prior to joining the institute staff in August 2017, Foote was the founding director of the Master of Science in First-Year Studies program, professor of education in the Department of First-Year and Transition Studies, and faculty fellow for high-impact practices at Kennesaw State University (KSU). Before joining the faculty at KSU, she served as the founding director of the Academic Success Center and First-Year Experience at the University of South Carolina Aiken and was the associate director for Student Orientation and Family Programs at Stony Brook University. Her scholarship and consultative work span a variety of aspects of student development and transition, including the role of first-year seminars and experiential pedagogy on student engagement in the early college experience, the community college transfer student transition, self-authorship development, engagement and learning in online environments, faculty development, metacognitive teaching and learning approaches, and high-impact educational practices. Foote is a recipient of the McGraw-Hill Excellence in Teaching First-Year Seminars award and a past recipient of the NODA Outstanding Research Award for her exploration of the effects of first-year seminar participation on the experience of students in the early college experience. She earned her PhD from the University of South Carolina in educational administration–higher education.

Gloria Gammell served as the inaugural project director for the Tennessee Reverse Transfer program while serving as the director of the University of Tennessee Kingsport Center for Higher Education. She began her career in higher education at the University of Kentucky as an academic advisor and has also served as registrar at the University of Michigan Law School, program administrator at

Siena Heights University (Michigan), director of student services at the East Tennessee State University College of Nursing, and director of the Weekend/Evening College at Virginia Intermont College. Gammell earned an EdD in higher education administration from Vanderbilt University, an MA in higher education administration from Eastern Michigan University, and an MA in sociology and a BS in psychology from Eastern Kentucky University. She retired from the University of Tennessee in 2017 after 37 years in higher education.

Maria L. Hesse serves as vice provost for academic partnerships at Arizona State University (ASU), helping to create and sustain productive relationships with community colleges and other organizations. Prior to joining ASU in 2009, Hesse served as president and CEO for Chandler-Gilbert Community College, one of the Maricopa Community Colleges in Phoenix, Arizona. She holds a Master of Business Administration from ASU, has master's and doctoral degrees in educational leadership from Northern Arizona University, and is a graduate of the Harvard Institute for Educational Management. She has served as a consultant to other colleges from Florida to California and is very active in a number of nonprofit organizations in the community.

Sonya Joseph is the assistant vice president for student affairs at Valencia College. She has more than 25 years of professional-level experience in student affairs. Joseph earned a bachelor's degree in math education from the University of Central Florida, a master's degree in higher education/student personnel from Florida State University, and a doctorate of education in curriculum and instruction with specializations in community college education and public administration. She has taught math, student success, student leadership, and career development at both the community college and university levels. At Valencia, Joseph led the college-wide redesign of student affairs, developed and implemented a professional development and training program for all student affairs staff, oversaw the Title III Pathways grant, and co-led the Foundations of Excellence self-study. She has also worked on the Achieving the Dream and Developmental Education Initiative teams. Her current work includes student activities, students with disabilities, and student system technology.

India Lane is a professor at the University of Tennessee (UT) College of Veterinary Medicine and associate vice president for academic affairs and student success at UT. Her professional background includes more than 20 years of engagement in veterinary education and seven years of service at the university system level. She leads cross-campus and statewide academic initiatives and oversees UT program and policy development. Prior to her current role, Lane earned a DVM from the

University of Georgia, an MS from Colorado State University, and an EdD from UT, Knoxville. She has held faculty roles at both the University of Prince Edward Island in Canada and UT, Knoxville.

Kristin Moser is director of the Office of Institutional Research & Effectiveness at the University of Northern Iowa (UNI). Prior to this, she served as senior research analyst at UNI from 2002 to 2015. She has a PhD in higher education from Iowa State University, an MA in psychology from Northern Arizona University, and a BA in psychology from UNI. In addition to Moser's role in Institutional Research & Effectiveness, she serves as co-chair for the UNI Transfer Council and the UNI Data and Research Council and provides leadership for institutional reaccreditation efforts through the Higher Learning Commission. She is the 2011-2012 recipient of the Paul P. Fidler Research Grant through the National Resource Center for The First-Year Experience and Students in Transition. Her work examined the development of capital for transfer students to facilitate successful transition and ultimately academic success at the four-year institution.

Kathleen Plinske serves as campus president of the Osceola, Lake Nona, and Poinciana Campuses at Valencia College in Orlando, Florida. Plinske began her career at McHenry County College in Crystal Lake, Illinois. She was hired as an instructional media specialist in 2001 and moved into a number of roles, including vice president of institutional effectiveness and ultimately, interim president. Plinske attended Indiana University-Bloomington as a Herman B Wells Scholar, earning a Bachelor of Arts in Spanish and physics with highest distinction and honors. A member of Phi Beta Kappa, she completed a Master of Arts in Spanish from Roosevelt University, a doctorate in educational technology from Pepperdine University, and a Master of Business Administration from the University of Florida. Plinske is actively involved in her community and has served as board chair of the Education Foundation of Osceola County and as president of the Rotary Club of Lake Nona. She has also served on the board of CareerSource Central Florida, the Osceola Center for the Arts, Junior Achievement of Osceola County, and the Lake Nona Education Council. She teaches the honors leadership course for Valencia College and graduate courses in educational leadership for the University of Central Florida and Pepperdine University. Plinske was named 2012 Woman of the Year by the *Orlando Business Journal* in its 40 Under 40 competition and the 2012 Outstanding Young Alumna by Indiana University. She received the 2013 Alumni Distinguished Leadership Award from the Illinois Mathematics and Science Academy. In 2014, she received the Compadre Award from the Hispanic Business Council of the Kissimmee/Osceola Chamber of Commerce and the Don Quijote Hispanic Community Champion Award from the Hispanic Chamber of Commerce of Metro Orlando. Plinske was selected as an Aspen Presidential Fellow in 2016.

Mark Allen Poisel is the vice chancellor for student affairs at the University of Arkansas at Little Rock. Serving as the chief student affairs and enrollment services officer at the university, he provides leadership, management, and supervision of enrollment areas, outreach and TRIO grants, student services and programs, and traditional student affairs functions. Poisel's prior work experience includes leadership positions in academic and student affairs at Augusta University, Pace University, the University of Central Florida, the Florida Department of Education, Florida State University, and Indiana State University. He has served as a keynote speaker at 16 conferences and symposia, conducted more than 65 presentations and workshops, and served as a consultant to other institutions of higher education on the topics of student success and strategic planning. He has published several articles and co-edited two books on transfer student success. He currently serves on the advisory board for the National Institute for the Study of Transfer Students and is a past board member of the National Resource Center for The First-Year Experience and Students in Transition. Finally, his teaching experience includes courses on individual and team leadership. Poisel earned his bachelor's in accounting and his master's in college student personnel work from Indiana State University and his specialist and EdD, both in higher education, from Florida State University.

Joyce C. Romano is vice president for educational partnerships at Valencia College, through which she works to improve the educational pathway for students from K-12 through community college and successful university transfer to bachelor's completion. Previously, her work at Valencia focused on the design and implementation of LifeMap, a developmental advising model and system; Atlas, a learning community portal; and the redesign of student services, which integrated student learning of educational processes to support their success. She has experience with diverse student populations and has designed and implemented programs for students from middle school through college graduation. Romano has a BA in psychology from State University of New York–College at Cortland, an MS in counseling psychology from Central Washington University, and an EdD in higher education from the University of Kansas.

Douglas T. Shapiro is the executive research director of the National Student Clearinghouse Research Center, which advances student success by providing the education community with data and insights from the nation's largest student-level longitudinal data set of college enrollment and degree information. The Research Center publishes annual reports on trends and benchmarks in student enrollment, persistence, transfer, mobility, and completion. The center also provides data services to measure student educational pathways for high schools, districts, states, postsecondary institutions, researchers, and other educational organizations. Shapiro has conducted research on students in higher education at the institution, state, and national levels. Prior to joining the Clearinghouse, he was the director of institutional research at The New School and before that, the vice president for research and policy development at the Minnesota Private College Council. He holds a PhD in education from the University of Michigan's Center for the Study of Higher and Postsecondary Education, an MA in mathematics from the University of Michigan, and a BA in history from the University of Chicago.

Carol A. Van Der Karr is the associate provost for academic affairs at SUNY Cortland. Her work over the past 20 years has focused on student learning and persistence, assessment, and academic support services. She holds a PhD in higher education from Syracuse University, and her scholarly interests are in organizational theory, student achievement, and institutional effectiveness.